Business
Strategy
for Success

**Principles for Strategic
Management of Business
Initiatives, Projects and
Programs**

By Russell Freytag

ISBN: 1530602068
ISBN 13: 9781530602063
Library of Congress Control Number: 2016904553
CreateSpace Independent Publishing Platform
North Charleston, South Carolina

Inquiries may be made at RussellFreytag2@gmail.com.

CONTENTS

PREFACE

Business Strategy for Success is a system developed to guide you in the creation and management of projects. It ensures that all of the life-cycle elements are covered when starting new initiatives, changing frameworks, reorganizing organizations, or working to make the company more efficient. The lead of the project will be in charge of all aspects of the initiatives, from the conception of the idea to measuring the success of the project. As companies are pushing for condensed timelines and reduced project life cycles, some of the principles in this book are not always clearly communicated by the transitional group owners or personnel such as business executives, IT executives, project management office (PMO), portfolio managers, product managers, program managers, or project managers, and some are being missed altogether. This book will teach you to increase the success rates of your projects by identifying the principles that drive successful initiatives and making sure that you have them assigned to the right resources.

This system highlights the importance of strategy when developing projects. Whether you are working with a sole proprietorship, a start-up, a global corporation, or a Fortune 500 company, this book will illustrate the steps that can be utilized to consistently achieve success. My methodology will allow the flexibility to use various frameworks, disciplines, and tools interchangeably in a repeatable model that will help to ensure success.

The past few years have brought an avalanche of applications and tools designed to streamline processes and enable more efficient program development. There has even been a push for standardized certification in the project-management profession. But however well intentioned, many times this has led to confusion in an industry-wide environment. This confusion does not, however, mean that the tools or processes themselves are flawed. Rather, it is how we are using these tools that is damaging and leaving us in a state of chaos.

The key is separating the tools from the strategy. There are many different frameworks that can be utilized to complete initiatives or projects, including Six Sigma, Lean, Waterfall, Software Development Life Cycle (SDLC), Project Management Institute (PMI), and Agile, just to name a few. These frameworks are commonly used by project managers who bring additional skills, tools, and knowledge to the project. All of these have variations that are utilized not only within companies but also within each department and even within individual teams. If such tools are used asynchronously, the project manager and team members will frequently have a different understanding of their roles and responsibilities. If everyone's strategy is not aligned, confusion will dominate the project.

Although the tools and frameworks will change depending on the project, the strategy is constant. This book will help you to make the distinction between strategy, tools, and framework. On some projects, you will be developing the strategy, and on some you will need to make sure you understand the strategy. But all strategies should have the high-level elements outlined in this book. A good strategy will remain the same and drive the team to succeed regardless of what tools or frameworks you use.

To be clear, all of these frameworks have good traits, but not every framework is right for every situation. Each project is different and will require different skill sets, talents, tools, and frameworks as well as its own approach. Again, although the tools and frameworks will change, depending on the program, the strategy will remain constant. A good strategy will remain the same and drive the team to succeed regardless of what tools you choose to use.

Business Strategy for Success defines the communication that will drive the project team to excel, regardless of what tools are being used or what the project may be. The most common problem that projects face is that every project runs differently, and there is not enough communication among team members about how and why they are doing what they are doing. Although the issues, problems, and teams are always different, the principles of strategy outlined in this book are a constant that have enabled me to consistently run successful projects.

I have included a symptom and pitfall section in each chapter of this book to help identify and prevent the most common project issues. This book will guide you to understand the importance of each step. It will also enable you to easily identify at what point an issue becomes a problem so that you can quickly return to that stage and make the necessary corrections or adjustments. After you have learned to use *Business Strategy for Success*, you will be able to not only run any project successfully but also have the ability to easily identify any problem and to diagnose issues within the project.

INTRODUCTION

I divided the book into three phases as illustrated in the diagram below.

Phase 1	Phase 2	Phase 3
Chapters	Chapters	Chapters
1. Strategy	5. Features and Functionality	9. Business Integration (Deploy)
2. Project Recovery or Rescue	6. Business Requirements	10. Measure and Future State
3. Management of Change	7. IT Data the Foundation	
4. Business Plan	8. Define the Framework	

The first phase requires that you assess all items in the book to ensure that you have a good understanding of the work ahead of you and of how to comprehend and develop your strategy. The book is heavy on the front end to ensure that you think through all elements of the project before you start working but enables you to taper the work down as you approach the launch of the program. This is opposite of the way that most projects run today, with little work done on the front end and an overwhelming amount of work due at launch. If this is a project you assess (a project that is in progress), you will decide if the project is a rescue, recovery, redo, or scrap. If the previous project manager has completed all of the steps to your satisfaction, you can continue with the project. You will be thinking about a plan to manage the changes that will be coming from the project, and, finally, you will be completing the business plan that you will present to the executive team to gain their approval to move forward. At the end of this phase, you will have a meeting with the executive team to determine if your project will be approved to continue—a go or no-go meeting.

In the second phase, you will be working with the customers to understand the features and functionalities that are required as well as developing the business requirements. In addition, you will be working to get pure data (raw, unchanged data) and you will have rolled out the framework you are using for this project. At the end of this phase you will have a second go or no-go meeting with all of the stakeholders to determine whether the project will be deployed.

In the final phase, you will integrate the project into the business to ensure acceptance of the changes. Then, you will measure the effects of the project against the expectations you set with the executive team to get the project approved. This is a step that tends to not get a lot of emphasis, since many times the next project is waiting, and there is little time to evaluate the completed project. I encourage you to utilize this step, as it will help you with future projects. And, finally, you will look at the future state and what changes may need to be planned for the project going forward.

Business Strategy for Success is the end-to-end life cycle for accomplishing key initiatives. The diagram below highlights some of the areas that you want to pay special attention to. Following the diagram is a summary of the contents of each chapter that covers one of these areas. I have often observed that these areas do not always receive much attention to detail and that the handoff to the next person or team is not always adequately performed or communicated.

Chapter 1	Chapter 2	Chapter 3	Chapter 4	Chapter 5	Chapter 6	Chapter 7	Chapter 8	Chapter 9	Chapter 10
Strategy	Project Recovery or Rescue	Management of Change	Business Plan	Features and Functionality	Business Requirements	IT Data the Foundation	Define the Framework	Business Integration	Measure and Future State

Chapter 1 discusses setting the strategy for the project, which is always a critical step. You should think through all of the other chapters and make decisions on the vision of the end state and define it in detail. This is one area that is consistently an issue and does not receive enough attention or direction when it is handed off to the next person in the process.

Chapter 2 covers the evaluation of a project that is in flight. Project evaluation is not done as often as it should be, and if it is done, it is at a framework level and not an end-to-end level. If you are taking over a project, you should make sure that all elements of the project have been completed to your satisfaction before you decide to move forward with the existing work that has been performed.

Chapter 3 discusses the management of change, which is not incorporated into all frameworks and is often missed completely. This is a huge issue when looking at the success of projects. Make sure you understand the current state of the business, have defined the future state of the business, and have a plan in place to manage the change of teams, roles, responsibilities, and processes from the current to future state.

Chapter 5 explains the importance of understanding and defining features and functionality in the business terms and working through the project using these terms to define the business requirements. Not doing this is a pitfall that many projects fall into. Working with the business and using its terminology will greatly enhance the participation and understanding of the project.

Chapter 7 emphasizes how critical it is to the success of the project to ensure that the data you are working with is untouched and pure. Using data that has been manipulated prior to your team's access to it will cause all types of problems down the road, since you will not have a true baseline of actual data to operate from. This is an issue that is often overlooked.

Chapter 10 covers the measurement of results against the strategy to understand the success of the program. This does not happen as often as it should. Rarely do projects turn out 100 percent complete with no additional work needing to be done. Understanding what additional work needs to be done and completing that work is not something that normally happens at the end of a project.

In the life cycle of projects I have seen, these are all issues that can cause problems. Thus, extra attention should be paid to these chapters to ensure that you get the best results possible for your projects.

Business Strategy for Success is not to be confused with the various frameworks that are used today as a part of completing projects. Certain frameworks will be mentioned in chapter 8 as part of the overall strategy to be used as needed. Some of the frameworks that I have used are Six Sigma, Lean, Waterfall, SDLC, PMI, and Agile. There are many variations of each of these, and I am not attempting to define these frameworks. This book will highlight the critical steps that should be taken to make a project successful. I give a brief description below of some of the frameworks to give the reader a high-level understanding of when it may be beneficial to pick one framework over another within the *Business Strategy for Success*. Keep in mind that each company, department, team, and team member may have a different understanding of each of the frameworks. The goal is to get everyone on the same page with the plan you choose to solve your business initiatives. I give a very brief, high-level description below of some of the frameworks for those of you who have not used them all.

Six Sigma is an analysis-based, quality-control framework that has been used successfully by many companies during the last thirty-plus years to increase the quality of products or processes. Lean is a framework that attempts to eliminate waste in materials, time, and uneven work distributions and to increase the use of technology or workflows. Six Sigma and Lean are sometimes linked and used as parts of the same framework.

Waterfall offers a structured development life cycle and is the most comprehensive of the frameworks. Its advantages are that it is easy to understand and manage but the downside is that it lacks flexibility for changes as you go through the project life cycle. To keep the business requirements relevant, it is best used for stable environments in which the customer's needs are well known and defined and for which project durations are an average of six months or less. The Waterfall framework may not work as well in situations in which business requirements are changing quickly and constantly.

SDLC framework also offers a structured development life cycle and also has limited ability for change, with a shortened life cycle starting at the receipt of business requirements to deployment (chapters 6 and 8 in the book) of the project. The cons of this type of development are that there is no structure for the first half of the project—strategy to gathering business requirements (chapters 1 through 5 in the book as well as chapters 7, 9, and 10)—leaving each business team to create its own process and structure. This often leads to steps being missed during this first half of the project, causing problems later.

Agile is the most flexible framework, offering quick cycle times (chapter 8 in the book), flexibility to adapt to rapidly changing requirements, and constant delivery to the business. The cons to Agile framework are that it is the most unstructured of the frameworks, with each team developing its own operating practices. This makes it a more challenging framework for management to adapt to, especially if they are coming from a more structured framework (Waterfall or SDLC) to Agile. Agile also relies on other groups or teams to do the other sections of the *Business Strategy for Success* (chapters 1 through 5 and 7, 9, and 10). Because of this, many of the principal elements of successful projects are not clearly communicated to the project team or get missed altogether.

Business Strategy for Success defines the principal elements that will drive your team to excel, no matter what tools you are using or what the project may be. The most common problem for projects is that each one runs differently and there is not enough communication among all team members about how and why they are doing what they're doing. Although the issues, problems, and teams are always different, the *principles of strategy* outlined in this book are a constant that have enabled me to consistently run successful projects.

After you have learned to use the *Business Strategy for Success,* you will be able to not only run a project successfully but also diagnose issues with your program, easily determine where the problem is, and fix it in real time rather than discuss it postmortem.

Throughout the book, we will follow a real scenario that occurred when a company's sales were flat for six straight quarters. The sales teams did not trust the reporting system, which had high error rates. They spent approximately 25 percent of their time tracking their sales and validating them against the reports instead of using this time to make sales. The sales teams' morale was low as a result of reporting being available only once per month with no way to validate their sales numbers prior to going to payroll for payout. Furthermore, the executives were unhappy with the sales performance but did not have a strategy to fix it.

AUTHOR'S NOTE

E ach chapter will begin with symptoms and end with pitfalls. These bullet points are designed to help identify and troubleshoot problems with the project. The symptoms are problems you may encounter. If you experience a symptom, align it with the correct chapter for assistance in identifying the cause of the problem. The pitfalls are the result of neglect. If you experience a pitfall, align it with the corresponding chapter, which will guide you to find the area that needs specific attention.

CHAPTER 1

STRATEGY

Symptoms

- Unclear or inconsistent communication and no understanding of strategic objectives
- Ambivalence about project goals with no plan to measure the success of the project upon completion
- Disorganization—lack of direction, focus, and productivity
- Executives questioning the program
- Lack of consistent communication of strategic objectives
- Team members uncertain about their new roles in the project
- Executives not engaged in the project
- Lack of measurable milestones for the project
- Ambiguity around roles and responsibilities—team skill sets do not align with new project needs
- Lack of engagement and commitment from team members

Determine Whether You Have a Project

The *Business Strategy for Success* will walk you through the steps that are necessary to evaluate whether you have a project. The steps covered in chapters 1 through 4 will help you understand the need of a project based on cost, priorities, and feasibility. Although it is tempting to skip these steps, the time and effort you spend on them will save you time and money later on. Emphasis on the steps contained in the first four chapters is critical to understanding what your goals are, and if your project is proven viable, these steps will work it through to a successful business or launch.

The Right Person to Evaluate Whether You Have a Project

It is important that you hire the right person to evaluate and determine whether you have a project. In order for this person to determine whether you have a project, he must be able to understand what it is you are wanting to accomplish and be able to analyze whether and how this process will be integrated into the existing business. He must align the partners to create a consistent flow of information, and he must have knowledge of what already exists in order to add to it successfully. Process knowledge is not enough. One must have institutional knowledge as well.

The person often chosen for this role is a *sales-type* personality. The inclination of some managers is to hire someone to sell their idea. But at this point, what are you selling? You haven't asked the right questions yet. The following breaks down what you want (on the left) versus what most people choose (on the right):

VISION	ENVISION
REALITY	FANTASY
FACT	FICTION

Before you commit your company to spending a lot of time and money on a project, you need to first have a vision of the process. The reality and facts of what you want to accomplish must be clear to all parties. You have to investigate and determine whether what it is you want to accomplish can actually be done. With booming technology and the fantasy of movies and the Internet, it's easy to overestimate the reality of what it is you want and what can actually be done. That's why it's important to choose a person who won't just blindly push your program but will do everything necessary to determine whether there is a project that can be accomplished. To simply envision a process of unproven fantasy and fiction will cause a lot of wasted money and time and many headaches.

Think of the structure of the military. The general in charge knows everything that is going on and how everything intersects and fits together. He is not leading people without the knowledge of what they do. He has institutional knowledge of everything that is going on under his command. Much like the military, where the battle field is always changing, business is constantly changing. Success requires a person who can see where the next explosion will take place before it happens. You need a blend of visionary discipline with the core requirements to fully understand as many as possible of the hundreds of tools, technological possibilities, and current functional requirements.

A good project manager is someone who will listen. You need to find someone with the knowledge of the business to listen to the symptoms, problems, and ideas in order to analyze the proposed project. From this analysis, she will be able to make the determination to go forward with the project or not.

Define the Methodology

Defining the methodology to be used throughout the project is not given an adequate amount of attention. Although this step can initially take a considerable amount of time, in the end you will not only save time but also increase your odds for success. The difference between starting a project and completing a project may very well be determined at this point. By mapping out your goals and setting the methodology for how you are going to accomplish them, you will move from the idea stage to the action stage and find that what you want to accomplish will happen.

Start with a breakdown of importance for creating a successful team. A project team consists of three parts that most people identify with: people, process, and technology. I have defined them a little differently below.

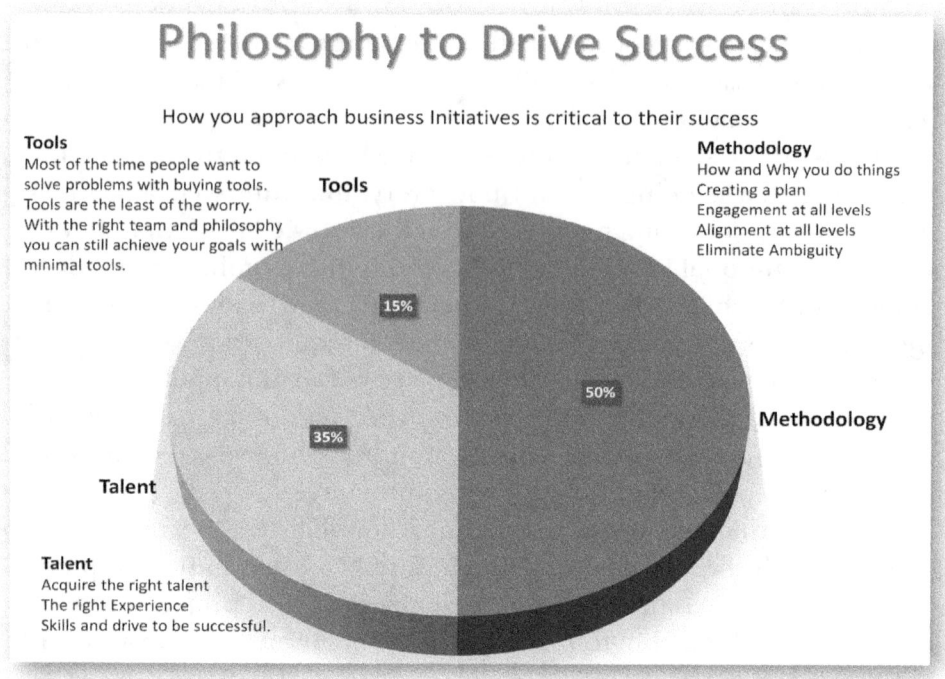

Philosophy to Drive Success

How you approach business Initiatives is critical to their success

Tools
Most of the time people want to
solve problems with buying tools.
Tools are the least of the worry.
With the right team and philosophy
you can still achieve your goals with
minimal tools.

Methodology
How and Why you do things
Creating a plan
Engagement at all levels
Alignment at all levels
Eliminate Ambiguity

Talent
Acquire the right talent
The right Experience
Skills and drive to be successful.

Tools — 15%
Talent — 35%
Methodology — 50%

Methodology and Philosophy

The methodology and philosophy of the team you put together to run your project is crucial to your success. Choosing people for your team needs to involve open communication, not only from you but also from the people you bring in. You must allow people to share their insights based on their experience and be willing to listen and trust their points of view. For a project to be successful, you cannot have a project manager who wants to do everything herself without listening to her experts. If your team does not feel like they have the ability to communicate openly with their team leaders, you will lose key information that will likely lead to the failure of the project or, in the best case, cost time and money that could have been saved. Bring in good people and trust your team!

Tie incentives to the success of the project. In a culture in which we don't want to assign winners and losers, how can you reward only success? A problem in many companies is that managers are rewarded not only for success but also for failure. People don't care whether a program succeeds or fails because they get their bonus or are promoted to the next project no matter what. It's win-win. Rather than pay for mediocrity, give people a reason to work for the success of the project. If you tie an incentive, at all levels, to the success of the program, people will be invested in that success. I am not advocating, however, that people be penalized for a project failure or bad performance, rather that the incentive be linked to the success of the project.

This idea also ties back to the original question, do you have a project? If your team is paid an incentive based on the success of a program, they are less likely to initiate a program that has little chance of success, because they would rather be working on a project that will add value to the company. Managers would not push projects just so they have something to do. They would be looking instead for the best projects and the best teams to carry them out.

Talent

You want to hire the best people you can find for the job, so choosing your team should be given careful thought. As many in this field know, working on a project can be an intense and personal experience. For a project to be successful, there must be absolute, open communication and an environment in which people feel free to think outside the box and introduce different ideas and theories. If they are working on a team that has people who are combative or judgmental, the creativity and energy of the team will suffer. Therefore, it is important that the team members you select are the best qualified for their positions and that they have the ability to create a close and open working environment.

Another point of consideration is the ability to keep a good team together. Although people who are experts in their fields can adapt to work within any team environment, it's definitely a bonus to bring together people who have a successful history of working with each other. The established communication among the team members will allow an increased ramp time and a better work tempo. The symmetry of an already established team can be a great asset to your project.

Think of a football team. Although the fundamentals of each position are the same, most would agree that the success of a team is highly dependent on the interaction of the people filling those positions. Skill and understanding will take you a long way, but the trust and teamwork that is acquired only by working together and knowing each other's abilities is what will make you win games.

Tools

Of least importance are the tools that a company buys and uses. This is contrary to what some people think. Companies spend millions of dollars on technology and tools for their operations but often fail to put the right teams together to operate the tools. Think about it. Most people have a computer, a smartphone, or another device of some sort to make the management of their lives easier. But many people use only a fraction of the capacity that such devices carry. We never learn the true capabilities of these devices because we don't take the time or effort to learn.

The same can be true for companies. They buy expensive tools to help with a critical process for their company but don't invest in the people who are running the tools. What tends to happen is that the tool is scrapped because nobody took the time to completely learn it. The resulting consensus is that the tool doesn't work or, at best, is underutilized. The people who will run the projects are more important than the tools. With the right team and philosophy, you can achieve your goals with a minimum of tools.

Define the Plan

Create the definition of your plan. What will make your project a success? This is a different question from, what is your project? This is not what your project is but how you are going to reach your goal of creating a successful project. The strategy for your plan must be high level, and the focus must be as tight as possible. You want to anticipate as much as possible and have a working timeline with measurable benchmarks to be able to evaluate your progress accurately.

These steps will be addressed in the following chapters but it is important to be aware of them and understand how they fit together. You are not working in a vacuum or on an assembly line. You must be aware of the whole picture.

Strategy

Strategy is the goal of what you are trying to achieve—the mission statement. In order to define what it is you want to achieve, you need a definitive mission statement. This statement must be as detailed and focused as possible. It is your constitution. Throughout the development of the program, you will be able to, at any time, refer back to the mission statement to keep you on track to reach your goal. It is easy to get sidetracked and turn your attention to other issues. Your mission statement will keep you focused and on pace.

The mission statement is also what you will use to gain executive support. Executive support is key; it is the lifeblood of any project. This cannot be stressed enough. If you don't have a clear mission that can be understood by management and every person on the team, the chances that your project will gain support above other projects are greatly reduced.

The mission statement should be clearly manageable. It should address the following:

- *Financial goals.* Set clear financial goals that align with company initiatives, that are realistic and measurable, and that will define the success of your program once you are done.
- *Cost avoidance.* Reduce costs that would have been higher if you had not intervened. For example, if you have a third-party vendor that performs a service for you, an analysis may determine that doing the work in house, utilizing existing personnel to do the job, may be cheaper.
- *Cost savings.* Take actions that allow the realization of lower costs than are projected. For example, if you currently purchase materials through a single vendor, then expanding to multiple vendors may allow you to realize cost savings by having multiple bids on the same product.
- *Revenue generation.* Take actions that result in increased revenue. These should be vetted through the finance department to ensure that the results are conservative and attainable. For example, if we increase the frequency of sales reporting and not only provide actuals but also include run-rate projections, this will motivate the sales teams to sell more product.
- *Automation.* Replace manual processes with automated processes. For example, reports that were completed by a person could be automated to run daily with rare or negligible human intervention. This would free up a person's time to act as a business analyst and interpret the data instead of simply running a report.
- *Reduction of personnel.* Removing non-value-adding processes and introducing changes in the business process to remove non-value-adding activities can reduce the number of people required to perform relevant processes. These people can be reassigned to other roles or projects that better utilize their time and skills.

- *Reduction of errors.* Address errors that can result in customer satisfaction issues as well as fix problems. Support fees and product replacements can be very costly.
- *Improvement of accuracy.* For example, increasing the accuracy of the order-placement process will have a cost reduction associated with it and can often be a key performance indicator for businesses.

Cost-Benefit Analysis

Once you have a clear mission statement, you will create the cost-benefit analysis (CBA). The CBA will outline the monetary benefit or loss realized by the company with the implementation of the process. The CBA should be a credible version of what the actual cost benefits will be. You should work with the finance team as well as all interested partners to create the most realistic report possible.

I use the words *realistic* and *credible* to emphasize the dangers of overselling your project's return on investment (ROI). It is at this point that the benefits may be enhanced in order to get projections that are desirable. Although this may be tempting, it is not recommended. You will be gaining executive support for your project based on the numbers from your CBA. A little variance may be expected, but if you stray too far from your number, you will quickly lose credibility and support.

In building the CBA, do not neglect to consider the costs associated with the business changes. Although the change details don't need to be completed at this time, the communication that a new team, in relation to the existing team, should be established while you are setting the strategy.

Here is a list of things to consider:

- new team organization versus existing team organization,
- new roles and responsibilities,
- new skill sets,
- new functions, and
- translation of skill sets from manual to automated needs.

It is important to define whether the project will be a local, regional, or global one. Determine whether it will be a scalable, transferable, or repeatable process. Determine whether technology and automation will be part of the solution. Assess the time frame that will be involved. All of these issues must be considered in building a reliable CBA.

Mission Statement

When creating a mission statement, many people will state only the obvious: what they want to do. This is why many projects fail before they've even started. To move forward before a strategy is set is like going on a trip without a map. You have a destination and just assume that if you point your car in the right direction, you'll end up there. Maybe you will and maybe you won't, but before you spend the time and money to make the journey, wouldn't you like a little insurance to make sure you end up in the right place? That's your strategy. If you don't take the time to outline a mission statement and build a strategy, then chances are you'll waver on the intent of your program and fail to achieve the goal you set out to reach. Time and time again, people choose to believe that the program will evolve into what they're aiming for, but do you really want to take that chance? I have not seen one example of a program simply evolving without a strategy into a working solution. It just does not happen.

Take the time to write out your mission statement and define your strategy. The work you do today will save you time, money, and headaches in the end.

Example Compensation Mission Statement

The objective of this program is to create a globally scalable, automated compensation tool and to reduce the current 15 percent error in compensation payout rate to less than 3 percent. The goal is also to increase the frequency of reporting from once a month to daily, with updates and run-rate projections specific to each sales rep. You also want to increase revenue by 1 percent for the first quarter, 1.5 percent for the next quarter, 2 percent for the next, and 2.5 percent by the end of the year due to the ability to drive behavior in the sales teams. Another goal is to change the current manual calculation process to an automated one, reducing the number of people needed to process compensation from eight to three. The three new team members will have different skill sets and operate at a higher level. The old team members will be transitioned to new roles. Additional divisions could be added by funding a business analyst. This system can be scaled globally due to centralizing the data and creating governance processes to align all divisions so that they are calculated in the same way.

Define Business Changes

You must address the issue of current team versus future team. When you have a process change or a new process being developed, most organizations will just defer to the team that is already in place. It is assumed that they will transition into the new positions created by the new process. In order to set up for your greatest chance of success, however, you need to look at the team dynamics and at each position as a specialty position. We discussed earlier the importance of choosing the right team of people to achieve your goals. Understanding the dynamics of what it is you are trying to achieve will help you make these decisions.

The skill sets needed for the positions you will be creating may be different from the skill sets of the people who are currently in place. If that is the case, you must bring in people who possess the skill sets you require. You must address the dynamics of the personalities and the cohesion of the team. Many managers don't address this because they feel it may mean that people will lose their jobs. To the contrary, this is exactly why this step is so important. By addressing these changes, you will proactively transition people who will be leaving the old process to areas that fit their skill sets. By actively practicing change management, these transitions will not be overlooked.

Some managers may find it easier to leave existing teams intact because they know the team and may have a comfortable relationship with them. But as you transition from the current state to the future state, consider that leaving the existing team in place can lead people to continue doing as they've always done. They may not adapt to the changes that are needed and may passively sabotage the project in order to pre-serve their way of doing things.

The State of the Business

Current state ➡ Transition state ➡ Future state

Current State

The main objective of this section is to find the root cause of the problem. This is different from the clutter of problems and complaints that the business may report. The root cause will not be complaints of poor communication or poor information flow. These are merely symptoms of the root problem. Finding the root of the problem requires digging into the processes and finding out what is causing the symptoms.

To accomplish this, you must know and understand the current state of the business. You need to know the people, positions, process, and technology as well as the roles and responsibilities. From this knowledge, you'll know whether the processes are manual, resource intensive, error prone, nonscalable, transferable, or sustainable. Is the team decentralized, inconsistent and unreliable, or error prone? Is there an allowance for business intelligence?

You must recognize the symptoms that point to a bigger issue in order to solve the problem. Many people don't see the need to understand the current state, and, therefore, they ignore it altogether. That's like adding onto a building without looking at the blueprints for the existing structure. How can you make the additions without knowing the foundation of the current state? Skipping this step can lead to the failure of your program.

Transition State

To define the interim state of the business, you must define the changes that will take place in the transition from the current state to the future state.

During this transition, you will define the organizational changes that will occur through the release and phases as well as all changes to the features and functionalities. You will make determinations of how the organization will change as the release occurs. Responsibilities for each phase will be determined, mapped out, and assigned.

Define the role changes by release and phase. You will need to diagram how the roles and responsibilities will change as you progress through the program. You will have to know what new roles are needed for the future state and how the existing roles in your current state will need to evolve in order to carry out the functions of the future state.

Future State

Your goal is to define the future state. To do this, you need to complete an end-to-end map outlining data, technology, people, process, and the business structure. You will define the goal and outline how it is going to be achieved. Besides the tools and process, you must define your future-state team. This will vary by the size and scope of your company, but there are some things to keep in mind.

Centralizing Teams

For smaller companies, this is easy. Your whole company is most likely located in one building. Many larger companies are becoming global, however, and they are allowing employees to work remotely or may have team members scattered in offices all over the globe. When companies take into account the dynamics or cohesion of team members, they may find that this could work them. More often than not, though, this decentralization of team members leads to the ultimate failure of a program.

When team members work together in the same space, the chances rise substantially that they will stay on track, work toward the same goal, and address issues as they occur. This leads to better team-member cohesion and better flow for everyone involved.

Leadership

Set the vision and identify the strategy to achieve the goal defined in the mission statement. You do not want to just wing it and hope that you succeed. You need concrete, tangible steps to ensure success.

Create the End State

You want to create the end state...the bull's-eye. You need to complete the end state with measurable financial information that you will validate in chapter 10. This statement will determine the success or failure of the program. This is the most important piece of work you will create, and, unfortunately, it is often overlooked. The more precisely you define the end state, the more likely you are to achieve it. Think of this as a target with concentric rings. Every time you define a measurement for the end state you create another ring. The more rings you create, the more you define the desired end state and the more likely you are to achieve that state. If you think about the task of an architect, you realize that the end state is exactly the same whether she is building a house, a commercial building, or a skyscraper. It is the definition of detail that will define the structure she is building. For the same reason, you want to use this detail in your business to get exactly what you want the first time. For our compensation example, we define success by adding as many definitions as possible to make sure we know exactly what we want to achieve and how to measure it when we finish the project.

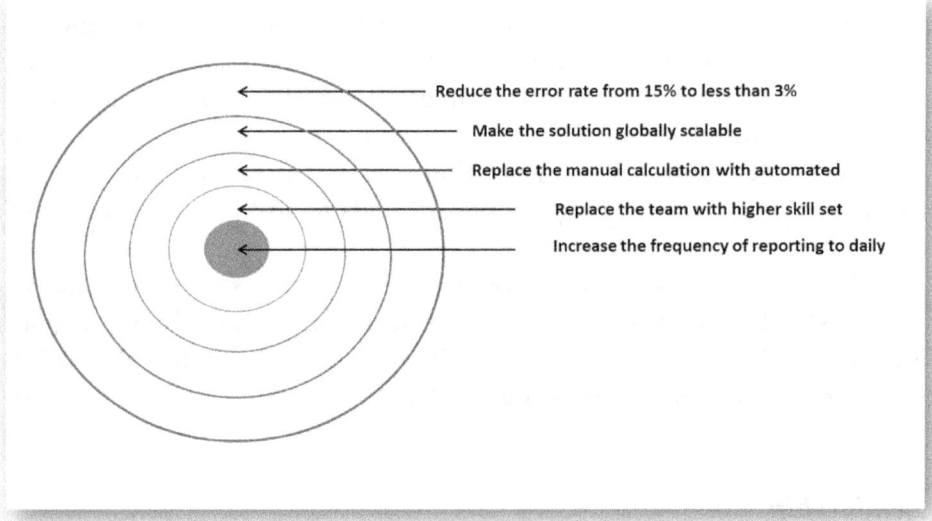

Reduce the error rate from 15% to less than 3%

Make the solution globally scalable

Replace the manual calculation with automated

Replace the team with higher skill set

Increase the frequency of reporting to daily

Executive Support

Executive support is crucial. The executives will decide what projects to fund. They will not fund your project unless you have sold them on it. This is why your plan, CBA, and analysis of current state to future state is so important. You must present a plan that lets the executives know all the components involved in going forward, including the cost benefits, time involved, and measurable financial and feasibility goals.

People are often in such a rush to get their project started that they don't properly prepare to get the executives buy in. Shortcuts may be taken, so you may not be properly prepared to present the plan and answer the questions that the executive staff will most likely ask. You don't want to let this happen. Often, you will have one chance to present your proposal; if you cannot sell it to the executives, you may not get another opportunity to do so. You are past the point of trying to sell a program based on good intentions and good ideas. You need measureable facts and projections.

You also don't want to oversell the executives on unrealistic projections. You should not underestimate the cost or the time involved, and you should not overestimate the cost benefit, because these are components that you can't hide forever. The true cost, the true amount of time, and the true cost benefit will eventually reveal themselves. If your deliverables and deadlines cannot be met, chances are you will lose your funding. The executives are basing their decision on the information you give them. Some cost or time overruns are usually expected, but if you're not even in the ballpark, the executives will lose faith in your plans, and you may lose a program that could have been of great benefit to the business.

Be brutally honest about all components of the program, and build a relationship of confidence and trust with the executives. This is how you will build a long-lasting relationship and be able to receive continued support for the project. We recommend that you meet daily, if possible, to keep them engaged with your program. After all, new programs are being proposed every day, and you want to keep them excited about what you are doing.

Like any other business function, executive support will vary depending on the size of the company you work for. In a smaller company, you will likely obtain executive sign-off only one time. After approval of the project, you will proceed without any concerns of losing that support. In larger companies, however, you may need to gain support from any number of sources. It may be a director, VP, GM, CEO, CIO, CFO, or a combination of these. In a larger company, you may have to continue the approval process throughout the life cycle of the project. This can be achieved with well-designed benchmarks throughout the project to validate the progress that is being achieved.

Another element that may affect support is the life cycle of the company you work for. If a company is growing and expanding, you will most likely gain more flexibility and support. But if you are working for a company that is losing its foothold in the industry and maybe contracting, then the support may be harder to come by. They will be watching every dollar, and, therefore, you will have to be especially careful about the cost benefit to the company. Executives may also be less likely to attach their name to a program because they don't want to have their name associated with anything that involves spending money or with something that has a possible risk of failure.

Knowing your company and your source of support can be invaluable. The decision of support may not always be based solely on the needs of the business but may be influenced by politics within the company. When you begin your steps in the strategy-for-success program, make sure that you are building your base as well as getting executive and political support for the program. This will also help you evaluate whether you have a project that is viable.

Define the Framework to Be Used

There are many options to think about when considering frameworks or practices to use for projects. For example, we can consider the case I introduced, a software development project. Waterfall is the traditional software-development practice that has been used by many companies. In my experience, however, it takes a long time to get from the business requirements to development to the launch. In this span of time the business may change, which can leave a less desirable solution. SDLC is a more recent development and has been popular among some of the larger companies. Its drawback is that it only provides a development option, which leaves the first half of the project with no business solution. This leaves the strategy through business requirements, chapters 1 through 6 of the book, undefined. Agile has been gaining popularity but may not be well understood across companies in general. Its appeal is the quick development cycles and constant delivery. Agile, too, has a downfall in that it provides even less structure, with every team moving in its own direction. This can be difficult for companies to understand, and they may have a hard time getting the productivity they desire. It will be your job to decide what makes the most sense for the project you are working on. Some companies allow for flexibility and some do not.

Keep in mind that these frameworks are only a part of the overall strategy for developing a solution. Thinking that these frameworks are the whole solution is one of the major mistakes that people make. (This will be discussed more extensively in chapter 8.)

For the compensation example, I chose to utilize Priority Matrix as the framework as well as Agile development with the business. I used these frameworks because they are most beneficial for the software that I was developing. (I will elaborate more on the Priority Matrix in chapter 8, since it is a lesser-known framework and can be extremely beneficial when used correctly.) Priority Matrix is more of an art form than an exact science. It is more along the lines of Agile development, and when utilized by the right person, it can be extremely beneficial.

Define the Team to Drive the Strategy

The following is a list of items to keep in mind when designing a project team:

- define the existing team with a future team,
- define the new organization,
- define the organizational structure,
- have executive support to make the changes,
- define roles and responsibilities for each team member,
- define whether you have centralized or decentralized teams,

- make sure the team you choose is committed to supporting the success of the team,
- hire the team,
- define each role in detail with a critical-to-core notation,
- set skill sets and core competencies,
- assess the project team,
- consider contractors and current employees, and
- consider recommendations from team members.

When forming the team, you should define each role in detail and establish the skill sets and core competencies. Try to avoid damaging the team by bringing in people based on favors or political agendas. This can result in hiring people who cannot perform the roles they were hired to do. Instead, rely on filling the required skill sets with the people you bring in. Don't limit your search for the best people to a small group of known employees. You may want to consider going outside the company to look at available contractors. Always be open to recommendations, and use all of the resources at your disposal to bring together the most qualified team possible.

Team Environment, Accountability, and Compensation

Have you ever worked on a team on which there was always a feeling of chaos and stress? Often, stress is the result of one person or a clash of personalities that just don't work well together, and their drama poisons the entire environment. This is not a team that will thrive. The team is so important, and you want an environment based on honesty and trust among the members. They must be able to speak freely and share ideas to create the best environment possible.

One problem I've encountered is employees hoarding their work. In many large companies, the environment is toxic to the extent that people are afraid to share their work for fear of it being stolen and then losing ownership of its success or for fear of being ridiculed for not performing as expected. Assume that you have a team of twenty people, and each person is doing his job but not sharing with the other nineteen people. How in the world can you expect this project to succeed? At launch, you just have to close your eyes, cross your fingers, and hope it works. In this type of scenario, even a single mistake can cause the project to fail.

The Cave

How can you structure and run your team in order to make it more productive and successful? One thing I recommend is "the cave." The cave is an environment in which your team members can work and be consumed in the project without the distractions of other business activities. It's important for the members to have daily meetings to touch base, update each other, and share the process of their work toward the end result. By meeting daily, people are up-to-date and can immediately address any issues that may occur. I've worked on many teams that were spread out, not only by building but also by locations. In such situations, access to team members may be limited, which can lead to issues and wasted work due to lack of communication. This can be devastating to the success of a project. For this reason, I stress the importance of keeping your team centralized, not only to one region but also to a designated room or area.

In today's global business world, people think it's great to form a team with people from the United States, India, South America, Asia, and so on. This may sound good, but the reality is that time differences as well as the inability to immediately resolve issues can hinder the progress of a project. There are many areas in which this diverse model can be effective in business, but running projects may not be one of them.

Compensation

Compensation is a touchy subject for many and therefore is not always addressed. In my experience, the most effective way to motivate people is to tie compensation to the success or failure of the project. In today's environment, people often don't care whether a project is a success or a failure since they get paid the same regardless of the outcome. I have seen teams go from project to project without a single one of them being a success. Ironically, they will receive bonuses and recognition for the very projects that have failed. This is extremely counterproductive. Give your people some skin in the game. If bonuses or rewards are tied to the success of the project, team members will be invested in that success and therefore will work harder to create it.

Skill Sets

When measuring skill sets at time of hire, most people go to the résumé. Does the interviewee have the required education or certificate levels to do the job? This may be a good standard to start out with, but you need to go further. Following are some skills you don't want to overlook.

- *Critical thinking.* One of the biggest problems in project management is the lack of communication skills. People routinely chase the symptoms of a problem rather than identify the problem itself. Your critical thinker will be able to identify the symptoms and, in turn, figure out what the core issue is and address it.
- *Listening skills.* You want a team of people who can listen to each other and create a project based on a high standard of communication.
- *Problem solving.* Having the ability to communicate, work together, and solve problems is crucial to any project's success. A project can be very complex, and you must have people who have the ability to not only solve complex problems at the core of the program but also maintain the fluidity of the project on a daily basis.
- *Project management skills.* Project management, unlike many roles in a company, takes on very different properties at different times. Accounting is a constant. Marketing is all about creativity, about thinking outside the box. Project management must be a little of both. You need to be able to understand and follow a complex program and, at the same time, be able to address the needs of the business as they come. Most people do not consider the complexities of a project. They may give you what they require but then a month in decide to change what they believe is a very small component. In reality, however, that small change

may take a lot of time and effort to alter and integrate into what you've already built.

> *Consider a person building a house. She wants her bedroom to face east so that the sun will wake her each morning. But the motel she is staying in put her in a room with an east-facing window, and she finds that she hates being awoken by the sun. So, a month into the project, she calls her contractor and wants to put the kitchen where the bedroom would have been. The foundation has already been poured and parts of the structure already built. It's not that easy for the contractor to make the change, but he must find a way to implement the change so that it will be structurally sound and also please the client.*

Core Competencies

Additional qualities that should be given consideration are the following:

- *Vision.* You want to have a shared vision throughout the team that is aligned to the same objectives.
- *Data analysis and reporting.* Analyze business data to be utilized for critical recommendations to senior staff decision-making.
- *Stakeholder management.* This refers to the ability to represent the interest of all groups involved and to understand their needs and objectives in order to incorporate their existing processes into the new program, which adds value to their existing programs.
- *Problem solving.* Be able to look at complex programs and work with business teams who tell you that they have problems but can tell you only what the symptoms are of those problems are and not what the problems themselves are. Instead of chasing the symptoms, you need to be able to find the root cause of the problems and solve them.
- *Change management.* Orchestrate the changes from the current to interim to future state while addressing people, processes, and technology.

- ***Process management and transformation.*** Understand the impact of your work and its consequences. Recognize how it enables others, but make sure you don't have an unintended negative impact.
- ***Business integration into the project.*** Work daily with each team member to make sure he understands his part in the project as well as how he fits into the overall project. Have executive engagement and support in making changes formal and accepted as the new standard for all organizations. Business integration will be used throughout every step of the book. It applies every time you have a new person or functional group enter the program. This is a step that is missing in many programs that will absolutely impact your ability to make changes to the business and be successful in your programs.
- ***Functional groups and extended team members.*** Work daily with all the functional partners. Communication, communication, communication!

This is part of change management. You should be able to understand all functional groups impacted by your program. Make sure to also understand their current-state processes as well as interim- and future-state solutions. Including these groups into the solution is critical. Without their input and buy-in, your program will not be adopted. Again, this is a critical portion of the program that is often overlooked and will cause problems later down the line if not addressed.

Pitfalls

- Not picking the right person to evaluate the project
- Not having a good plan (strategy, execution, measure) and training a core team to follow the same methodology and philosophy
- Not having clear goals and being able to communicate what will be achieved by the project in the short-, medium-, and long-term phases
- Not having an established financial reason for the program
- Not clearly defining the end goal of the project with measurable criteria for success
- Not creating a change-management plan for the project
- Not securing executive support for the project
- Not defining the framework, milestones, and documents to be used for the project and integrating the team in this plan
- Not hiring the right people for the job (looking at people as resources and not individuals with very specific skill sets that should be aligned with the needs of the project)
- Not securing the bandwidth of key resources so they can be 100 percent utilized on this program

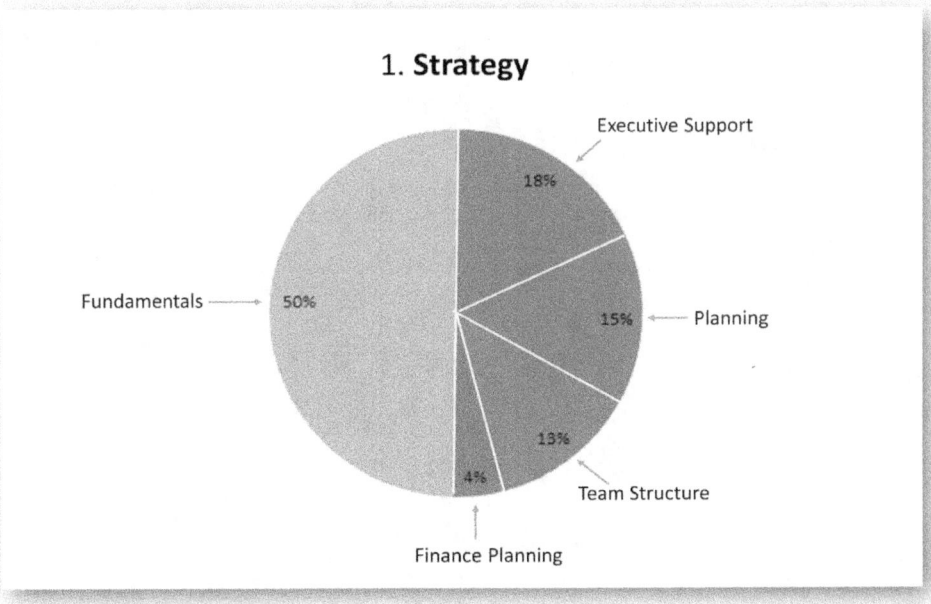

1. Strategy

Executive Support — 18%
Planning — 15%
Team Structure — 13%
Finance Planning — 4%
Fundamentals — 50%

These graphs at the end of each chapter give a visual of the time allotment given to each discipline throughout the life cycle of your project. As you advance through the chapters, you'll notice that the time allotment will shift and change according to your phase of the project.

The bulk of your time is spent on the fundamentals of the project. The fundamentals represent the base of your work, the platform that everything else will be built upon. You'll also devote time to gaining executive support, planning, and designing team structure, and you will begin to consider finance planning.

CHAPTER 2

PROJECT RECOVERY OR RESCUE

Symptoms

- Executives questioning the program or constant issues between the project team and the business team that don't seem to get resolved
- Project has been operating for an extended period of time and has stalled because of general lack of interest
- Poor communication between the project team and the stakeholders
- Person running the project disengaged and not communicating with the team on strategy, vision, and plans
- No clear understanding of what has been done on the project
- Team members unsure of the goals and purpose of the project
- Executives questioning the need for the project

T he symptoms of a recovery are about the problems with the initiative itself. A stalled process or a general lack of interest are good examples. All of the following are possible symptoms.

- The program has been operating for an extended period of time without the expected or desired results.

- The program has stalled because of a general lack of interest.
- There is renewed interest in a program by the executives.
- Executives are questioning the purpose of the project.
- The program is being launched in order to check a box.

The symptoms of a rescue are more about the people involved with the program. What they do, or fail to do, can drive the program to failure. Symptoms could be

- poor communication between the project team and the stakeholders;
- infighting between the project team and the functional groups over deadlines, capabilities, and deliverables;
- the dreaded blame game (people planning who to blame for the project's failure);
- people critical to the program changing roles or leaving;
- stakeholders having little or no input in the program; or
- control issues (constant issues and infighting among the groups).

Although rescues and recoveries each have distinct characteristics, it's important to recognize that there are some issues common to both. These include the following.

- There are control issues, and there is constant infighting among the groups. Everything is an issue or nothing works.
- Things are not well thought out. Your strategy may not have been fully vetted.
- Objective-based tracking of issues has stopped, and thus stakeholder/core-team meetings are no longer productive.

Following the steps laid out in chapter 2 will allow you to evaluate whether you have a rescue or a recovery program and how to move forward.

Recovery or Rescue Program

When setting out to determine whether you have a rescue or a recovery program, it is imperative to have good communication and the right people to make this evaluation. You must have a project manager who is given the trust and commitment to thoroughly evaluate any project that is in a recovery or rescue phase. He cannot be expected to report only what management or the business wants to hear. The PM must have the ability to report any and all problems with the current program.

The PM will make the determination to continue with the current project or to start it over. This is not an easy position to be in. He may receive a lot of pressure to continue the project even though that may not be what is best for the business. Some people may take offense to the implication that what they are building is not working or is in trouble. They may perceive any change as a threat and may fight anything that looks like a change to the status quo. Management may feel that starting a project over is unnecessary and may elect to work through the problems instead. Beware, however, that if you continue to move forward with a damaged project, you risk wasting a lot of time and money. You may end up in a never-ending loop that prevents you from accomplishing the goals that were originally envisioned.

> *Assume you own a car that turned out to be a lemon. You may love the car for its style, but if you are constantly having to take it in to the mechanic for repairs, it will become a burden. What's worse is if you can't determine the root cause of the problem. You will continue to spend time and money on a problem that you may never solve. At some point, you must make the decision to get a new car that will be reliable.*

Besides listening to your PM, you must establish the stakeholders. Stakeholder management is critical at this stage. Make sure you take the time to truly understand who the stakeholders are and listen to them. At this point, everyone is jockeying for position and wants to define the project. Make sure you recognize the subject-matter experts (SMEs) within all the functional groups and develop a strong relationship of communication with them. Keep the focus of the project on track, and don't be distracted by the "busy noise." This establishment takes time and should be worked on daily. This is part of the change-catalyst role that the visionary usually holds. You have to understand all of the stakeholders' roles and responsibilities, needs, and expectations.

Part of the communication will be to pull the team back together and focus on the facts. You want to rank the issues and always have your critical issues as the focus. Take the personal pieces out of the project and concentrate only on the facts. How you communicate the facts of the issues is critical, and how they are communicated back to you will be key to your success. Focus on the good work that people are doing. At this point, positive reinforcement can be used to rally your team.

You must set the right expectations with the executive team. This is vital. Executives are the drivers of all programs, and your relationship with them, as well as your ability to set goals and expectations for them, is crucial. You have to be brutally honest in setting expectations and mapping out a project plan that can succeed. Ignoring issues or glossing over areas of concern may lead to the failure of your project.

People will follow a good leader. Lead by example. Work harder, listen longer, and have more patience. If anything, over communicate. This is the only way to bring a rescue program back to life. If necessary, win the people of the team over one at a time by working for them and not talking down to them. Strong-arm tactics will not work and will most likely backfire. A PM may fail at this point if she continues to drive in the wrong direction. She often will not take the time to listen or to work with the stakeholders. She may drive to the date and not consider a rescue. Try to avoid making that mistake.

If you are taking over an existing program, you should start again at the point of defining the strategy. You cannot start with new people taking over an existing program. The amount of time it takes to integrate new people into the program is not available. Depending on the project, it can take months to bring people up to speed. Be careful that key people are not run off by people that have no idea what the program is or what it's about. Be diligent that the right people are put in positions of ownership.

You hired the PM not only to run the project but also to evaluate it for issues of rescue or recovery. Allow him to do his job with security and open communication. He may tell you what you don't want to hear, but he will tell you the truth and save you time and money down the road. You will establish a relationship of responsibility and trust. Failure to set the right strategy with the right vision will end many projects in the same way that misleading the executive team in order to gain their support for the project will ultimately backfire and fail.

Differences between Recovery and Rescue

Project Recovery
A project recovery is necessary when a program that has been in development for some time is unable to find its footing because of lack of executive support, lack of direction, or lack of a plan. These symptoms can cause a project to feel never-ending. Without clear goals, people come in and do their jobs, but nothing seems to come of it. There are a variety of reasons for this stagnation. The project may have value but no one wants to take responsibility for it. Funding may be an issue. It could be a political project designed to keep a department busy. Whatever the reason, this is a project recovery.

Once a project recovery is identified, you must treat it as a new project. You cannot assume that the current work is reliable. You must set up the goals and expectations, establish the executive support, and start over.

Project Rescue
A project rescue is a program that is in full project mode but has developed issues that may cause it to fail. These issues may be the departure of core people, the reorganization of the team, or a change in the philosophy of the project. When a core leader leaves, she is usually replaced, and the project continues. The new person will not have or understand the objectives previously laid out for this project and many

times will want to make it her own. This not only damages the work that has already been done but also jeopardizes the integrity of the previous goals.

Evaluate the Team

Once you have determined whether you have a rescue project or a recovery project, you need to evaluate the current team. Do you have the right team in place to make the project a success? If your project is in rescue or recovery mode, then probably not. Following are some questions to consider.

- Did the team have executive support?
- Did you have the right team members?
- Did the team have a clear goal or objective?
- Did the team have a cohesive vision?
- Was everyone working in sync to reach their goal?
- Was there strong communication among the team members?

Companies often make the mistake of reorganizing but keeping the same people on the team as the project is refocused. The reasoning is that they are already familiar with the program, and, therefore, time is saved that would have been spent bringing new people up to speed on the project. The problem with this philosophy is that it's difficult for people to change. They may not understand or agree with the reasoning behind having to change their focus or how they've been doing things. This will also lead to shortcuts. People will feel that they have already done the work and should not have to do it again. This will leave you vulnerable to repeated mistakes. In the long run, this will damage the project and may lead you to a repeated failure.

You should evaluate the new roles and responsibilities that are needed and find the right people for those positions. The best person for each job will have institutional knowledge as well as the ability to work well with the other team members. You want to create a team that is dedicated and is invested in the success of the new program.

Evaluate the Project

You must evaluate the project and fully understand where you are in the project life cycle. Once this is determined, you will need to ensure that all of the steps were completed in order to make the project a success. Failing to do this step inevitably leads to problems because you have no idea where the project is and what has or has not been done up to that point.

Determine the Methodology and Philosophy

Determining the methodology and philosophy is a step that is often ignored. What does it even mean? This is a step that with some thought and planning will save you countless headaches in the long run.

The methodology and philosophy you choose will define how you want your team to be organized. In today's global environment, a team may have members working from almost every continent. Many people choose to work from home while others may work hours that fit into their schedule and may be available for contact only at certain times of the day. Technology is a wonderful thing and is great when everything comes together. When developing a project, however, you must have team members plugged in. Constant communication is imperative. Their work and ultimate goals depend on them having access to one another and working together. This cannot be done if the team members are not working in a common environment.

This methodology is up to you and will depend on the structure and reliability of your employees. Some teams who work remotely are able to obtain a good system of communication with great success. The goal of the team may be more strongly defined and attained, however, when the members are working together with strong communication and access.

When I worked for global corporations, it was not uncommon to work with people from all over the world. Scheduling meetings was doable and, with today's technology, fairly effective. The problem I encountered, however, was real-time communication. If one of us had an issue needing immediate attention, it would sometimes take twenty-four hours or more to make contact with the right team member, which created a drag on the process. If I had been working with someone on-site and couldn't reach them by phone or e-mail, I could have simply walked to their work space and dealt with the issue immediately.

Operational Plan

When you are evaluating a project R3S (rescue, recovery, redo, and scrap), all the operational aspects must be reviewed. Whenever you take over an in-flight project, the first thing you should do is evaluate what has been done to date. That includes understanding exactly what phase the project is in, whether it has skipped any steps, and whether you are in a position to continue the project without starting over. It is very unlikely that all aspects have been covered and that everything is up-to-date. If that were the case, the project would most likely not be transitioned to a new owner. Refer back to chapter 1 to review all the operational aspects to evaluate during this chapter.

Establish a Clear Vision Statement and Strategy

At this point, you will have established exactly what kind of project you will be working on. You will recognize the project as a new project, a recovery, or a rescue. You will have put a team in place with clear roles and responsibilities to complete your objectives. Now is the time to establish a clear vision statement and strategy.

A strong vision statement and strategy will solidify the purpose and goals of the project. Each of us tends to have unique perspectives, but, as a team, we must create and work toward the creation of a strong program. You must intertwine your abilities and responsibilities so that your goals come together to meet all of the objectives. If the team members do not have a good understanding of the vision and strategic goals, the project will ultimately lose its definition and focus. Without a vision statement, the original strategy will be lost and what will be left is a team doing busy work with no clear goal or objective.

Start Over or Continue with Current Project?

Answer the following questions.

- Are you aligned with the company's strategic initiatives?
- Do you have a clear strategy for this program?
- Have you defined your methodology and philosophy?
- Are you solving the right problem?
- Do you have a clear understanding of what the real problem is?

If you cannot answer these questions, then you are not clear on all the objectives. If this is the case, then you need to work with your dedicated executive sponsor to reset expectations for the project and start from the beginning.

Pitfalls

- Not managing the risk of the program
- Not having executive support and engagement for the project
- Not having the right person run the project
- Not securing the right team for the project
- Not evaluating the project to make sure all steps were completed before proceeding with the project
- Not fully understanding all stakeholders and the current-to-future state with a full gap-analysis bridge
- Not aligning with company initiatives

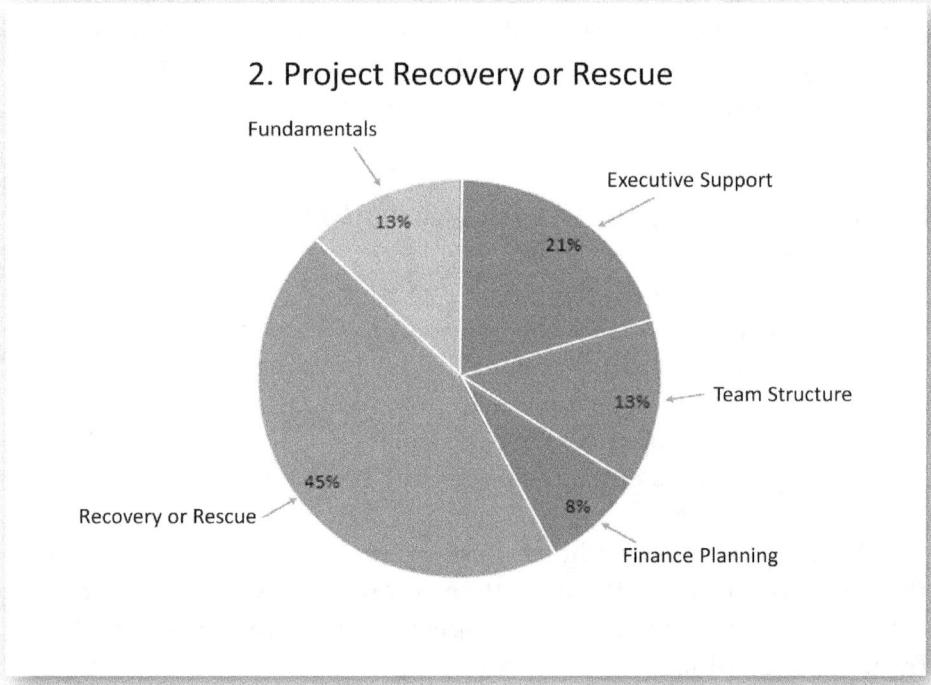

2. Project Recovery or Rescue

Fundamentals

Executive Support

13%

21%

Team Structure

13%

45%

8%

Recovery or Rescue

Finance Planning

In chapter 2, you have spent time determining whether your project is a rescue, recovery, redo, or scrap. You continue to gain executive support and align team structure with a little gain in financial planning. You are reviewing the fundamentals to gain alignment on what was completed on this project, and you will make a decision on whether or not to proceed or to scrap the project.

CHAPTER 3

MANAGEMENT OF CHANGE

Symptoms

- Organizational or structural process changes stalled—lack of engagement from executives
- Confusion around purpose—no clear objectives identified
- Inability to tie specific features and functionality to the CBA
- Lack of communication
- Confusion surrounding roles and responsibilities as they relate to the change occurring
- Too much time spent in meetings
- People confused as to what their new role will be
- Deteriorating communication between the project team and the business
- Current business structure does not support new process

The issues below are leading indicators that course correction should be considered.

- No change catalyst is assigned to the program.
- Executives have not signed off on organizational or structural process changes.

- Project time lines are dictated by the executives.
- People in roles are not allowed to do their jobs.
- Scope creep…good and bad.
- There are too many meetings in which time is wasted.
- Messaging around the project is not cleared or approved by the core team but is delivered by executives that are disengaged from the core team.
- There is no executive scorecard detailing the specific features and functionality time lines along with the CBA estimates.

Lagging Indicators

The lagging indicators are issues that may be slower to present and therefore should be given special consideration.

- You are not achieving the efficiencies you set out to achieve.
- Manual-to-automated process ratios are off.
- You are working with empire builders, not business drivers.
- Managers and leaders resist change.
- Executives are not involved or engaged.
- Current structure does not support the new process.
- Management styles are ineffective.

The Management of Change

The management of change addresses many of the issues discussed in chapter 1. If you have already addressed these issues, then you are ahead, and this step will strengthen what you have already done.

The management of change is the act of transitioning from the current state of your process to the future state.

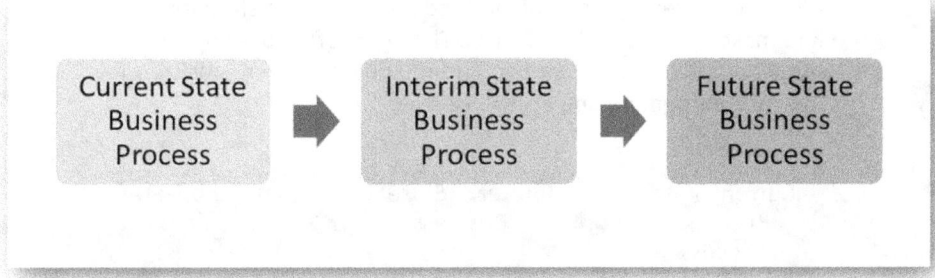

Once you have defined your goal, create the strategy that will move you from the current state into the future state as seamlessly as possible. To make this transition, adjustments and allowances must be made so that the current-state process can be used until the future state is tested and ready to take over all the functionalities without interruption to the business.

Many people do not understand the importance of knowing the current state of the business when planning to implement a change to that system. After all, they are interested in changing the current process, so why bother with how it was? When the change is decided, duties are often distributed among team members without analysis of what the needs and requirements will be for the new program, much less of how they will handle the transitional phase of the project. Rarely are new processes seamlessly transitioned so that they are turned on at the same moment old processes are turned off. When evaluating the current state of a business, one must consider that generally the processes being performed today are being performed for a reason. This means that all the steps in the current state need to be identified and categorized into three buckets:

1. *Automate.* You will be automating the process.
2. *Change the business.* You will be changing the business in a way that makes the step irrelevant.
3. *Stay the same.* Someone has to continue to perform this process.

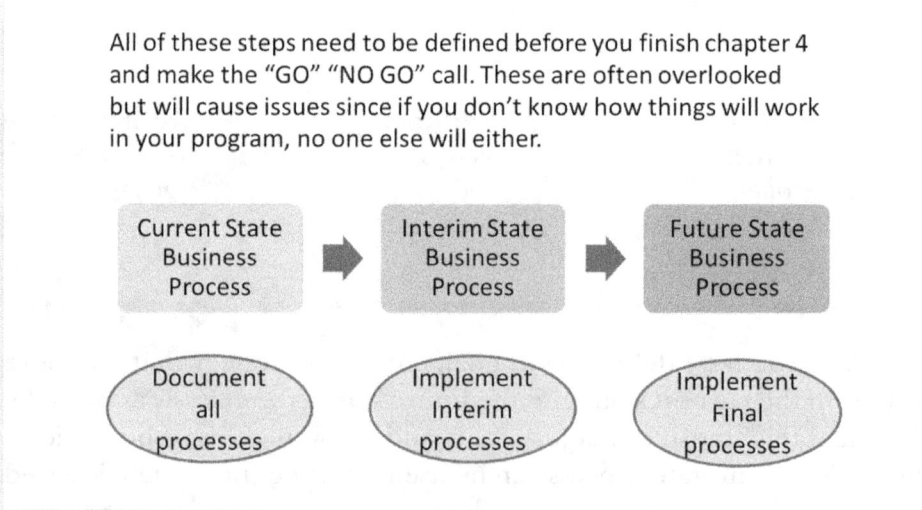

All of these steps need to be defined before you finish chapter 4 and make the "GO" "NO GO" call. These are often overlooked but will cause issues since if you don't know how things will work in your program, no one else will either.

Current State Business Process → Interim State Business Process → Future State Business Process

Document all processes / Implement Interim processes / Implement Final processes

You need to analyze what your new team will look like. If you're changing from a manual-process system to an automated system, for example, your team may require fewer people. The requirements for new positions will likely require broader skill sets than those of the people currently making up the team. Many programs may fail because changes in staff have not been considered, and, as the program progresses, issues may occur between the new program teams and the current team. The current team may not want to adapt to or have the skill set to perform the new processes. These ownership changes need to be identified and agreed on before you start the project.

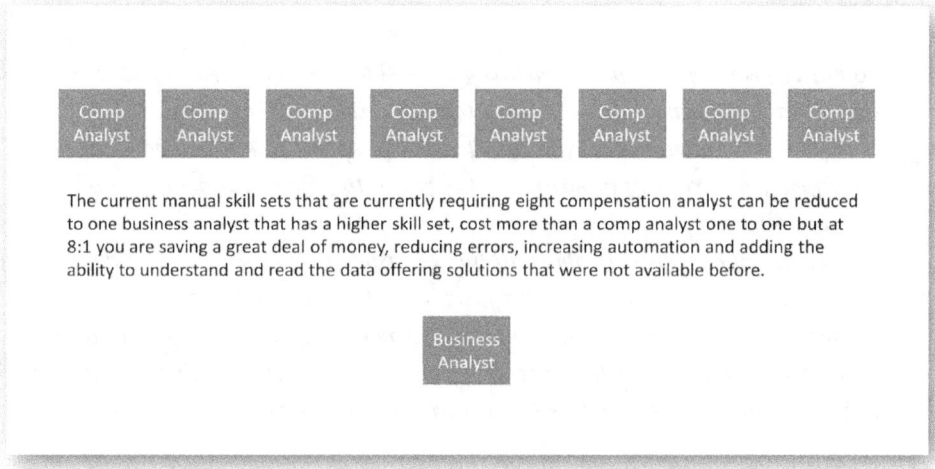

The current manual skill sets that are currently requiring eight compensation analyst can be reduced to one business analyst that has a higher skill set, cost more than a comp analyst one to one but at 8:1 you are saving a great deal of money, reducing errors, increasing automation and adding the ability to understand and read the data offering solutions that were not available before.

Finding the Cost Benefit

Have you defined the benefits of the new structure? There are a lot of questions you must consider, and this is one of the first and most important to answer before you go any further. What are the benefits? Why are you creating this process, or why are you changing an existing process? What benefit will you gain? Only after answering these questions will you begin to understand what benefit there may or may not be.

Benefits and Costs

Once you determine what the benefit is, you must determine the cost of the benefit. When doing your CBA, you will have to determine if the cost benefit is sufficient to justify the funding and implementation of your plan. If the benefit is not sufficient compared to your cost, you will need to rethink your strategy of moving forward with the project. Your CBA will be key to obtaining and sustaining executive support. The executive team works in numbers, and if the cost does not justify your project, the executives will turn their attention and support elsewhere. Make sure you have a solid and accurate CBA if you want to gain executive support and keep it.

> *So many people just want something new. They're so excited about starting a new program that they don't take the time to think about the cost; they just plow ahead. But you don't want to spend one hundred dollars on a new and exciting program that is going to give you a benefit of only ninety dollars.*
>
> *Think of coupons. People will buy products they don't even need just because they have a coupon and have the opportunity to "save" a little money. Are you really saving money if you're buying something you don't need or will not use? Is the purchase justified? No. And neither is a new program that has not been vetted out and proven to be a cost benefit.*

Change Catalyst

The change catalyst is the person that will work with all levels of operations to make the changes needed to integrate the business. Depending on the size of your program, you may need change catalysts at all levels of the business. The project manager will need to be in constant communication, and the change leads should be an extension of his vision, with constant integration into these leads. The change that takes place as you are implementing your program must be a well-thought-out and planned event. Everyone in the program must know how the change is occurring and what their part is in it. If they don't know why or how things are changing, then they won't be able to give you feedback on the progress or on any potential issues. Constant feedback from your SMEs is a must. Communication must be constant at this point to ensure that everyone is moving in the right direction.

Identify the Size of the Program

How do you identify whether a project is too large for one PM and will require multiple project managers? When a project becomes too large for one person to manage, two things will occur:

1. You will lose the ability of team members to communicate issues directly to the project manager.
2. You will lose the ability for the project manager to communicate issues directly to the team members.

If you lose the ability of team members to communicate issues to the PM, you lose the ability to be the expert or the visionary of the project. You simply do not have the necessary information to do the job. Likewise, if you lose the ability to communicate your vision with the team members, you will be detached from the contributors. It is critical that everyone understands what they are doing and why they are doing it. You must be aware of the warning signs that occur when a project has become too big for one PM. Fully defining this is critical in the strategy phase.

Change Management Implementation

Change management is the process of transitioning from one process to a new process, from the current state of the business to the future state of the business. You must plan for every phase of the transition. How will the current state be managed during the development of the future state? How will the transition be handled after the implementation of the future state has begun? What will the future state look like compared to the current state? How will the current state be phased out once the future state is fully implemented?

All these questions must be addressed and answered in order to have a smooth transition. The steps you put in place must be managed and constantly changed or adjusted as deemed necessary. Ignoring the transitional phase from current state to future state will highly increase the number of issues encountered during this process, wasting valuable time and money. You must remember that all the phases—current state, transitional state, and future state—are equally important. You must plan every transition and handoff of duty. You can't do this if you don't know the current state or how you are going to make changes to get to the future state.

> *Consider the remodel of a house. You can't just take a picture and magically own a new home. You first must know the current state of the home. What dimensions do you have to work with? Where will the electrical outlets be? Where is the plumbing connected? Do you have gas lines? These are the structural issues you must know in order to plan your remodel effectively. Now you need to answer the logistics. Will you move out during the remodel or simply move your living area from room to room until you are finished? Will you be able to use the kitchen or bathroom facilities? Finally, you must consider the transition and how you will reestablish your routine. Does your old decor fit your new living space or will you need to replace it?*

The issues dealt with when outlining the change management will prevent the excessive costs that plague many projects. You are taking the process of change into consideration, recognizing the transitional change, and creating a more accurate CBA to work with.

Define the Plan

Keep in mind that the events discussed in chapters 1 through 4 are all happening at the same time. Business integration is needed for the operational, structural, organizational, and technical changes.

You must analyze the current situation to make sure, once again, that you have the correct actions outlined in your strategy and that you fully understand what you are trying to achieve. You must define the organization and changes to be implemented as the project progresses and develop a plan to implement the changes that includes working with the executive team to ensure alignment.

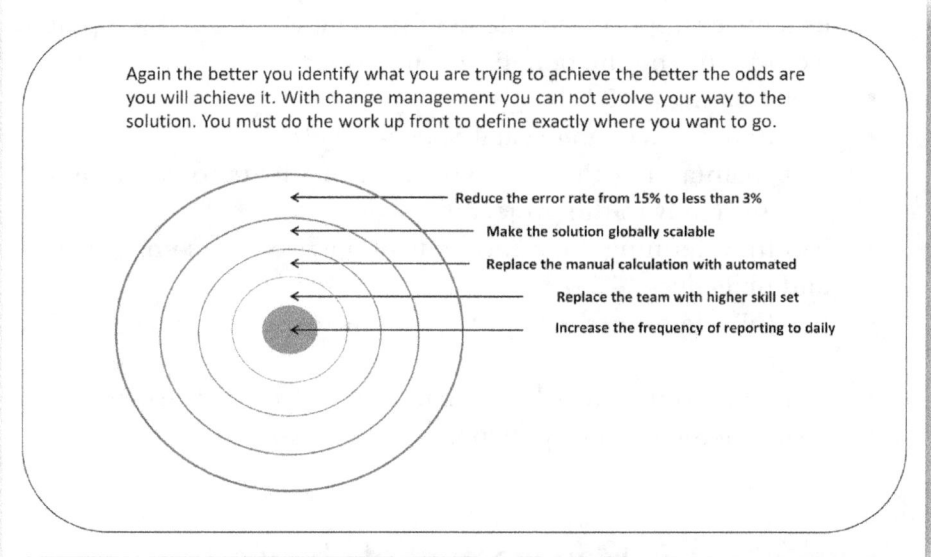

Again the better you identify what you are trying to achieve the better the odds are you will achieve it. With change management you can not evolve your way to the solution. You must do the work up front to define exactly where you want to go.

Reduce the error rate from 15% to less than 3%

Make the solution globally scalable

Replace the manual calculation with automated

Replace the team with higher skill set

Increase the frequency of reporting to daily

Deploy the Change

Change does not come easily. Many companies will continue to run costly, outdated processes because it's more comfortable than making a change. Or, worse, a company may decide to update or change its process but will sabotage its success by continuing to revert back to old ways.

In order to successfully change or implement a new process, it is important to follow the guide outlined for you. You must outline a clear, consistent plan to keep you within the parameters of the change. You must implement communication at all levels and between all of your stakeholders. You must have consensus with your executive team and set expectations for all phases of the change.

You cannot move forward on the assumption that your business will naturally evolve into a new, more efficient program without proper planning and direction.

Pitfalls

- Not defining the change that will be occurring and not getting executive support to implement the changes from the top down
- Not identifying the benefits of the project
- Not creating a CBA
- Not defining a change catalyst at all levels
- Not maintaining the ability of team members to communicate issues directly to the project manager
- Not fully defining the future state of the project, team, processes, and objectives
- Not fully defining the objective and the expected outcome of the project
- Thinking your team will automatically evolve into the new process
- Overlooking current-state business processes

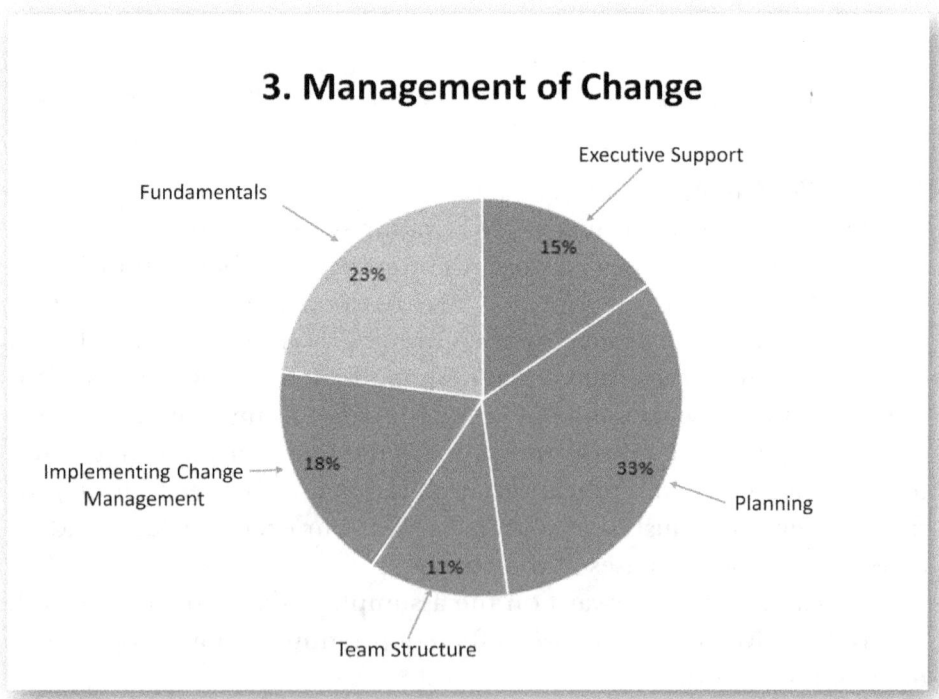

Planning has become your main focus, with the fundamentals continuing to be an important component of your time. You will begin to work on change management at this phase as well as continue interest in executive support and team structure. Finance planning has become a sliver but is still an important component that you should not disregard.

CHAPTER 4

BUSINESS PLAN

Symptoms

- Goal of project constantly changing
- Problems with the business plan and CBA—no input from finance or other key stakeholders
- No executive support for the project
- Confusion of the problem—the scope continues to increase
- Confusion of organization, processes, roles, and responsibilities
- Inability to produce a business plan for validation
- Financial impact is inconsistent with CBA
- Stakeholders starting to disengage from the project

Business Plan

Following is a review of what has been completed in chapters 1 through 3.

- Setting up the strategy
- Identifying the program
- Getting the right person to evaluate the program
- Defining the methodology and philosophy
- Defining the plan
- Understanding the current state

- Defining the interim state
- Designing the future state
- Obtaining executive support
- Defining the team
- Identifying recovery or rescue program
- Defining the right team for the type of program
- Establishing a clear vision statement and strategy
- Defining a start over or a continuation of the project
- Defining the management of change
- Defining your strategic transition from current state through interim state to the future state
- Identifying a change catalyst
- Defining the plan

You should now have a solid business plan that covers all phases of the project. The plan will outline strategy, current state, interim state, and future state as well as roles and responsibilities, business support, executive support, and all lines of communication.

All components needed to complete a thorough CBA should now be gathered and available.

Finance Business-Plan Designate

A finance business-plan designate will analyze the business plan and determine whether the plan is financially sound. There are many reasons for this analysis. The bottom line is that if it takes more money to build the process than the benefit realized, you should not go forward with the program. Too often, the idea of a project gets ahead of the ultimate purpose. Companies see a need for a solution without taking the time to determine not only whether they can afford it but also whether the plan will actually save or generate the dollar amounts expected.

Choosing the right person to analyze and build the CBA is crucial. This person must rely strictly on the numbers. Ideally, you will want to bring in someone who has no ties to the project. It cannot be stressed enough that at this point you don't want politics or an agenda—you just want the numbers. If you are a smaller company, however, you may not have the resources to bring in someone who is not tied to the project. It must simply be stressed that the decision must be objective and not agenda driven. The key is to let the facts speak for themselves. Do not try to manipulate the outcome of the CBA. If the numbers are not there, don't force it. Take it for what it is—a tool that will guide you in making sound decisions.

Once you have completed a detailed, vetted CBA and a business plan, your executive support will have the information they need to make the decision to continue and implement the program or to shelve it. A project with positive cost benefits may be immediately put into play or, based on the company's needs, may be ranked among other projects competing for funds. Either way, the CBA will be tested. If it has been completed correctly, then it will be supported by the findings.

Example Compensation CBA

The following is a very high-level look at a cost-benefit analysis. A lot of work and detail has gone into validating the categories to be measured. This includes work with the finance designate that is not reflected by this high-level look and the addition of vendor funding to supplement some of the sales compensation. Such additions are possible when the sales teams are selling the products of vendors and the vendors are paying a bonus to the company for achieving sales quotas. Not all companies can utilize this, but it is worth looking into. Also, in some cases, vendor dollars can be utilized to pay taxes of products sold. Your finance or accounting department can help you with the correct way to handle this regarding payouts and accounting.

Currently, sales have been flat quarter after quarter. Sales reporting is completed a month after the sales month closes, with no time to review payouts prior to submitting to payroll. The error rate is in excess of 15 percent, which has caused morale issues with the sales teams. They spend a sizable amount of time tracking their sales on spreadsheets rather than selling, because they do not trust the reporting.

Cost Benefits Analysis

Sales Teams	Current state sales reporting creation and support	Future state sales reporting creation and support
Reporting time to release	Reporting is one month in arrears	Real time report generation / modeling
Incremental opex	$0	Vendor funded
Tax breaks	$0	Vendor funded
Incremental FTE's	0	2
List all FTE's required for sales reporting	8	3
ROI	Impossible to calculate	6.75% annually or $337,500
Lost opportunity cost	-337,500	$337,500
Flexibility	Changes monthly. Manual / error prone	Allows for changes on the fly
Additional opportunity cost	Not scaleable or sustainable	Scalable to all sales teams globally
Additional opportunity cost	Manual support	Centralized IT support

Define the Problem

Within the business plan, you have defined the current state, the interim state, and the future state of the business. Now you will add the financial impact to all of the steps. You need to marry the cost-benefit analysis to the business plan, which will allow you to quantify where you're going along with the cost or savings realized. This is what you need to solidify in order to retain executive support for the project.

Remember that some people may not bother with the current- or interim-state knowledge. Instead, they keep their focus solely on the future state. This mistake may lead to project failures because these components are not figured into the CBA and are therefore not accounted for.

The business plan, CBA, and real-use cases in other areas illustrate what you can achieve. The finance partner will keep you grounded and will address the root cause of a problem rather than chasing symptoms. Define every functional group affected by the current problems and quantify the current state of the business.

Things to consider are

- effects of head count reduction
- moving from a manual process to an automated process,
- cost savings and cost avoidance,
- revenue generation,
- tax breaks, and
- vendor contributions.

Define the New Organizational Needs

Define the organizational needs for the program. The needs of management, as well as the required skill sets and core competencies, must be addressed. Every part of the organization that is touched must be analyzed for its needs. A good tool to do this is a time-in-motion study.

A time-in-motion study utilized at this stage is a good measurement of the program and can be part of the mission statement. Use this as a way to capture the transference from current state to interim state and through to the future state with the CBA numbers attached. Once again, you can see that having a clear plan of current to future state is critical to assessing the true cost involved. Team changes, current state, interim state, and future state, as well as the final stages, must be defined.

You must also recognize what the change is going to be and how that change will affect the organization. Determine whether you are replacing a manual process with automation. Understand how the future state will change the organization. The time-in-motion study will link these steps. It will find and reveal any gaps you may have overlooked.

The teams involved in the transition from the interim state to the future state must not only have the skill sets required for the job but also have the direction and freedom to challenge the status quo. It is important for the development of the program to have challenges at every level. You want managers who encourage feedback and team members who feel free to speak up and point out issues and concerns. Open communication is a must.

One thing you must be careful about is how much involvement is given to the business. The business should be involved, but it is important for finance, operations, and other parties to provide the proper governance for projects. For example, the new process may be phasing the current business out, and, therefore, participation by the current team could be a conflict of interest and may be a concern. You want to ensure that your project assumptions and findings are unbiased and validated by a third party, not just by one group.

Example of Time in Motion

The current business should not be responsible for the time-in-motion study. It should be done with a designated team or the finance team to measure the results and to validate findings as the project moves from current-state to future-state processes. The current time-in-motion study shows that it takes eight resources to support this very manual, error-prone process that so far has been unable to produce any increase in revenue over the last several quarters of sales.

Time in motion study
Prior to launch manual process

Current state error rate	>15%
Number of times sales reports are run monthly	1
Average number of reports run monthly	60
Time it takes to set up and run sales reports	30 plus days
Increased revenue opportunity	$0
Total headcount to support the program	8

Financial Analysis and Impact to the Business

Define your financial analysis. Now that you have completed the business plan and the CBA, you will complete a full, detailed analysis to determine whether the goal of the process can be achieved. Determine whether the projections are realistic and address all the costs, revenues, and savings that will result from the implementation of this program. Any gap that may be in the business plan or CBA should become apparent and should be addressed at this point. It is the detail and specifics you gain here that will solidify support for the project.

Go or No-Go

This is the point that, with clarity, the decision will be made to go or no-go. Will you proceed forward with the project or stop here? A no-go doesn't always mean dropping the entire program. The company may put it in a queue of future projects or, based on projections, may wish to retool the idea and go in a different direction.

The important thing to remember is that the data you've laid out will lead to the best choice for the project. You don't want to build up a project based on inflated numbers only to begin a new project that, financially, will bring no benefit to the company.

How many times have you heard of or been involved with a new project that spun into major cost overruns? The project will inevitably be scrapped, resulting in a loss of not only money but also time. At best, it may limp along with an inflated price tag. Either scenario is not good. Companies cannot afford this type of wasteful spending. Although cost variances are common, if you follow the steps I've laid out, you will be able to limit any surprises.

Besides cost, the business plan and CBA will determine if you are solving the right problem or merely chasing a symptom of the true problem. Don't get caught focusing on the wrong issues, and don't be afraid to meet a problem head-on. Keep in mind that, for some, problems can mean job security. If they are chasing issues, they may be searching for a way to show their value. This can lead to the loops I mentioned. People don't always want to change and may create chaos to avoid doing so.

The following is a list of other things to consider.

- Stop looking at the road maps for corporate planning and start looking at a new model for projects.
- Determine what you want to get out of this project.
- New models for the project teams need to be established.
- If you run a project team, you should have the ability to add and remove people.
- Your team is your people…choose them wisely.
- You cannot afford to not do this process.
- Pitch to the solution.
- What type of tools are you using for the CBA?

Pitfalls

- Not planning the project thoroughly
- Not partnering with finance on the CBA
- Not doing a CBA
- Not correctly identifying the root cause of the problem you are trying to solve
- Solving the wrong problem
- Not defining the new organizational needs
- Trying to make a project for which there is little or no cost benefit
- Overstating the benefit of the project
- Not including all stakeholders in the go or no-go meeting

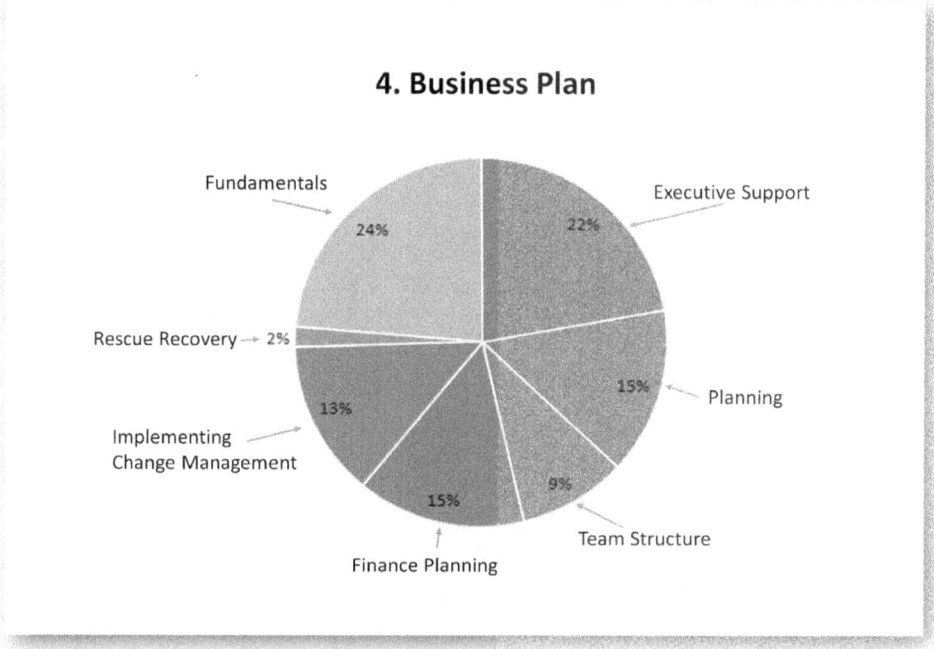

At this important juncture of go or no-go, fundamentals remain a strong priority in making this decision. Executive support will also be a strong contributing factor. Planning, finance planning, and change management will all be factors of consideration, with team structure and rescue/recovery requiring a little less attention.

CHAPTER 5

FEATURES AND FUNCTIONALITY

Symptoms

- Lack of understanding by the business of the language used to describe features because they are identified in technical terms
- No clearly documented features and functionalities by functional group—stack ranked from top to bottom prioritized by functional group
- No ability to communicate what the future-state features or functionality will be because there is no common understanding of terms
- Executive support hard to gain because financial benefits have not been defined
- Complaints from the business that what is being delivered is not what is being asked for
- A lack of consensus and understanding of current state
- Inability to understand the impact of current-state issues as they relate to the full life cycle—confusion over issues that arise
- Gaps in coverage of roles and responsibilities
- People concerned about what their changing roles will become

Features and Functionalities

One problem in business today is the lack of definition of the project manager. Many project managers are neither technical nor business but are scribes for the business. The business may have an idea of what it wants but may be reacting only to the symptoms of the problem. A good project manager will be able to look deeper than the symptoms and identify the root cause of the problem.

The business may also have a lack of understanding of the process that will be needed in order to achieve its goals. It doesn't help that IT speaks a different language and may have a hard time translating the needs of the business into a workable solution. The project manager will be the interpreter between the business and IT. Communication is critical and must be assisted by someone who has a working knowledge of both the business and IT.

The project manager should possess the ability to determine and map out the needs of the business. These needs will be conveyed to IT in a manner that allows IT to build out a plan with features and functionalities defined in the business language. This is important. If the terminology used in building out the process is not that of the business, it will lead to confusion and problems. It is vital to the success of the project that the terminology be written in the language of the business.

During the evaluation and design of the transition from the current state to future state, the project manager will map out the process with all of its features and functionalities. The project manager must identify all functional groups that will be affected by the process and account for the changes in the most efficient manner possible. With a long-running project, you will need to reassess the business to determine whether you are maintaining all the functional groups and successfully meeting their needs.

When mapping out the process end to end, it is important that the current state, interim state, future state, and features and functionalities of all functional groups be linked to the CBA with tangible results and accountability built into the process. If you tie the CBA to the features and functionality as you start the priority matrix, you will have a tool to keep the executives engaged in the project with measurable results.

Compensation Example

Working with finance, you can now assign monetary values to the features that you will be adding during this project. The diagram below represents the expected benefit from releasing the new features. Tying monetary values to each feature helps keep the executives engaged. We have specific modeling, however, that we are not sure how to put a value on. This may prove to be more valuable than we expected. We placed the value on all the items up to modeling and left this as a bonus since we expect this will hold a high return for the business. Modeling can reveal the compensation that is implemented today, but it can actually be detrimental to the business. I suspect this is the case in reviewing the current compensation plans. We will only know the value of the current compensation plans once this project is implemented.

Deployment Order	Features to Implement	Dollar Benefit Gained from this implementation
1	Single Source of Data	$10,000
2	Automated Sales Rep Level Reporting	$10,000
3	Automated Pay file Generation (Cash in Paycheck)	$17,500
4	Leader Boards	$100,000
5	Automated Sales Contest Generation	$100,000
6	Sales Rep Dashboard	$100,000
7	Compensation Modeling	This is where the value kicks in.
8	Return on Investment Calculation	Unable to put a value on this
	Total Benefit	$337,500

Validation with All Business Partners—Needs and Priorities

Mapping the process and making sure that all functional groups can be accounted for can be a painstaking step that is often skimmed over. But making sure that you have identified everyone who will be affected by the process will save you major difficulties and possible failures in the end.

To start the mapping process, you need to identify every input into and output from the flow. Draw it out. You want to literally create the map of your process. Next, take the full list of functional partners identified on your map, eliminate the obvious, and contact the remaining to confirm their part in the process change. If you are not sure of all the partners, you can start with the department heads to identify the inputs and outputs throughout their departments.

As you identify the functional groups involved in the process change, you will need to select SMEs in each area for all of the processes that will be affected by the change. Communication must be established between the project manager and the SMEs to confirm that all the features and functionalities are being captured. It can be helpful to stack rank the business functionalities. You must have all parties aligned with a clear understanding of what you are trying to achieve written in the functional language of the business.

Understand the Current State of the Business

Having learned the current state, you will work with the business to initiate a time-in-motion study. By understanding the current state of the business, you will be able to quantify the interim and the future state. At this phase, the project plan will need to identify whether the steps are being done to correctly deliver the business needs. You will need to build in and capture key points in time. You will identify phases, delivery points, pilot, release, or combinations of these. Key milestones will be added to measure progress throughout the project.

Document Current-State Process for All Groups Involved or Affected by the Change

Once you fully understand the current state, you will document the current-state process for all of the functional groups. A complete, high-level, down-to-the-details development will be needed to make sure all elements are incorporated.

It would be helpful to organize all the current-state processes into buckets: automate, change the business, and continue manual, for example. All of the processes must be accounted for as you move forward. You need to quantify the processes and start working on the interim process that will be needed as you move through the final phase: the future state.

Tie the process maps back to the strategy statement and the CBA to quantify the savings by phase as part of the strategy statement.

Document Current-State Roles and Responsibilities for All Functional Groups

One important area of attention is the definition and documentation of roles and responsibilities. Many companies rely on meetings and divide the duties to cover work assignments. This can be a mistake. You want to fully document what people are doing as part of the time-in-motion study. From this study, you will quantify the processes that will be changing in the future state and at what phase the changes will occur. The roles and responsibilities must be defined throughout all the phases of change. The organization will need to be defined as part of the strategy statement. The better the strategy is defined, the higher your chances for success.

Define the Integration Plan:

The following is a list of points to consider when defining the integration plan.

- Define the roles and responsibilities for each phase.
- Make sure you have executive support to execute the plan.
- Define a change-management and the management-of-change plan.
- Work through the plan constantly with all the business partners.
- Maintain a good understanding of the business.
- Communicate with all the business partners in the language of the business.
- Keep executives engaged as you move through the project, especially with projects that are long term (six months to a year or more in duration).

Pitfalls

- Not defining the features and functionalities using the business language in one pager and a two-to-four pager and not detailing specs that may be a hundred or more pages
- Not assigning monetary values to the features and functionalities being delivered
- Not identifying all functional groups impacted by the project
- Not fully understanding the current-state business functionality
- Not fully understanding how all functional groups work together in their current state
- No ability to see the big picture, the full life cycle
- Not documenting current- to future-state roles and responsibilities mapping
- Not creating a future-state plan for all groups affected by the project changes

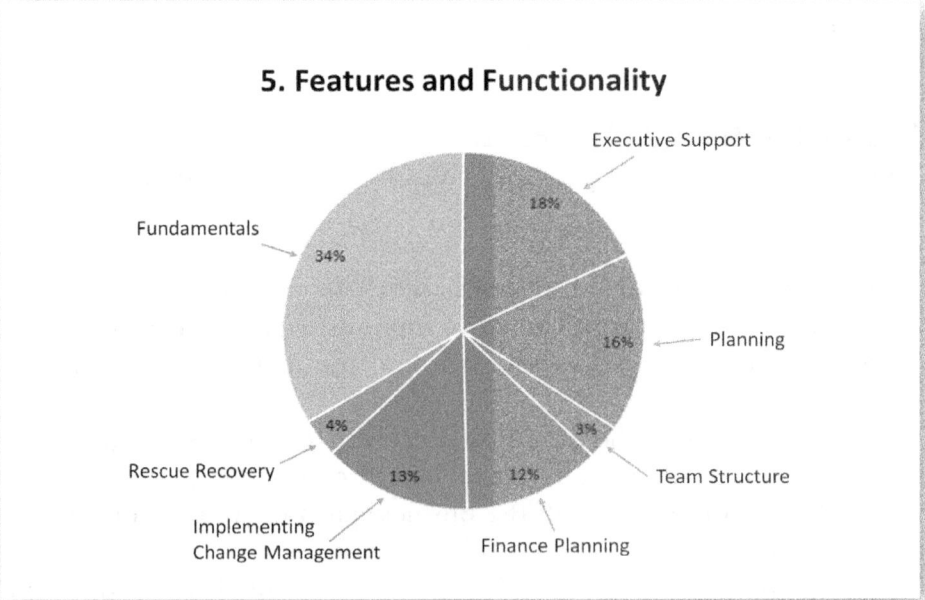

5. Features and Functionality

- Executive Support — 18%
- Planning — 16%
- Team Structure — 3%
- Finance Planning — 12%
- Implementing Change Management — 13%
- Rescue Recovery — 4%
- Fundamentals — 34%

As you work through features and functionality, you'll see that fundamentals increases in time allotment once again. Executive support and planning continue to be priorities, with change management and finance planning still requiring some attention at this phase. Rescue/recovery and team structure will still be considerations, but less time is allotted here.

CHAPTER 6

BUSINESS REQUIREMENTS

Symptoms

- Business not clear what the requirements are because they are defined using technical language
- Business has no understanding of technology options that are possible for the project
- IT team unclear about what the business is trying to achieve for this project
- No clear communication about future state of the project is coming from project team
- No future-state processes have been documented or defined
- People confused about what their changing roles will become
- BRD does not represent needs of the business because it was written by someone that does not represent the business

Creating the Business Requirements Document

The business requirements document (BRD) will entail a high-level list of features and functionalities that will be written in the business language and will tie back to the CBA. Ideally, the BRD will be guided by, if not written by, the SMEs. From the features and functionalities that have been identified in chapter 5, you should be able to quantify the business requirements.

Detail requirements will expand the list of features and functionalities and provide greater detail to the document. The business will write the requirements to ensure that its needs are being met. But it must work with an IT person to make sure that what it wants can, in fact, be done. Through this process, you will accomplish the following items.

- Create a detailed description of the feature.
- Determine who will be impacted.
- Determine what applications will be impacted.
- Create mock-up or screen shots to illustrate what it is you are trying to create.
- Define role-based capabilities by functionality.

The BRD can be illustrated in a menu-style example. The high-level requirements are the menu items. Each item listed represents a product that must be produced. The detail requirements symbolize the recipe for each item—everything that must go into the menu item. But the depth you must go into to outline the process requires more than simply having a recipe. What are the ingredients? Where do you get them? How and by whom are they being prepared? What do you serve your products on? Will you use disposable or washable plates, cups, and utensils? How will you store your raw ingredients before they are prepared?

These are all detail requirements that must be mapped out in order to complete the BRD. All the requirements will have a cost associated with them and must be tied to the CBA. This will also answer questions about roles and responsibilities. You must define who will be responsible for all of the functionalities you are creating.

You can begin to see how all of these issues tie together. Nothing can be done in a vacuum. Every step has accountability to the structural integrity of the process.

Business Integration with the IT Organization

It's important for the person writing the BRD to do so working side by side with an IT partner. As you gather the requirements, the IT partner will have a full understanding of exactly what the business is trying to accomplish. With this understanding, IT can steer you to make sure that what you want is technically possible. Also, by working together with you to gather the requirements, IT will have a clear understanding of the goals and objectives as well as of the business language that is needed.

Imagine you are preparing to build a house. But instead of hiring an architect or meeting with the builder, you simply provide a list of requirements. Your list states that you want three bedrooms, two baths, one kitchen, a den, and a fireplace. In your mind, you picture exactly what you want. But does the contractor interpret your requirements in the same way? Are all three bedrooms the same size? Is the den a living room or an office? In what room do you want the fireplace? What size is the kitchen to be? The contractor may use his kitchen only to slap together peanut-butter sandwiches, so he may feel a very small kitchen is adequate when you were picturing a large, gourmet kitchen. You can begin to see why clear interpretation is important in writing the requirements. Communication and detail are key, especially with IT. They will guide you to the most effective ways to accomplish your goals and help you avoid the pitfalls.

Technical Feasibility Discussion with IT

Admit it: in this day and age, with technology so prevalent in our lives, many of us think we really know and understand all aspects of technology. This assumption can prove to be wrong, however, when dealing with process flows. When the business is trying to fix a problem, it often addresses the symptoms of that problem rather than targeting the true issue.

The business must work with IT as a partner who will guide it to identify and understand the root cause of the problem. A good partnership can lead to open discussions that will help IT understand their value in providing guidance to solve the issues that the business is experiencing. IT will evaluate how things are done with the existing technology, processes, and tools. They will analyze and determine new, innovative ways to solve any problems the business may be encountering.

Documenting Future-State Processes and Gap Analysis

Working through the business requirements with the IT partner should highlight the importance of understanding current state to future state with a gap analysis of the business. Recognizing a change that is fluid, that is always moving from the current state to the future state, is imperative. The focus now should be on the gap analysis. How do you get from point *A* to point *B*?

The gap analysis is the interim phase of the process. It refers to all the gaps that occur as you are building and transitioning from the current state to the future state. You want to be careful not to have "blackouts" occur as you are changing the process. You do not want to lose business as you are trying to build a better business. Therefore, you must plan strategy to cover the gaps as you build in the changes and improvements.

> *Think of a road-improvement project as an example. You can't just shut down an existing road to make improvements without offering a detour to avoid impeding traffic. A well-thought-out plan provides a detour that takes into consideration the ease of transition and continued access to established businesses on the route with the best mobility possible. This will keep businesses from losing customers and also create an ease of traffic that will protect the possibility of future business.*

This is your gap analysis. You must protect the current productivity at the same time that you transition the business to the future-process procedures.

Defining Roles and Responsibilities

The future state is what you are working toward, so be sure to plan accordingly. Don't wait until you are in the future state to decide details such as roles and responsibilities. This can be a huge pitfall. To ensure a successful transition, you must tie the roles and responsibilities to the change management, gap analysis, and current- to future-state maps. The roles and responsibilities must be specifically and decisively defined.

As time-in-motion studies are completed and the outline confirmed, they will be utilized throughout the program until the process is completed. When a new team is being created and the ownership and roles and responsibilities are changing, the time in motion studymust be documented for all phases and states of the business. The roles of the current-state team will be different from the roles of the interim-state team, and those roles will be different from the roles and responsibilities of the future-state team.

The better you organize, communicate with, and prepare all the parties affected by these changes, the better the transition will be. The management of change must be clearly identified, mapped, and communicated at every level.

This step sounds good and sensible, but it is one step that many people avoid. The idea is that a changed organization means that many jobs as they are today will be dissolved. This will scare many, and they will cling to the old ways in order to preserve what they have. Rather than avoiding this fear, you need to prepare your gap analysis and clearly lay out a plan for roles and responsibilities throughout the entire process. If you communicate and share the plans, people will be on board and able to contribute to the change (because they will know what their role is) and will not continue to do as they have always done. If the people on the current-state team don't understand the change and don't see their role in it, they may sabotage the program, and you may never have a chance of success.

Risk Management

Understanding and identifying risk will be an ongoing process throughout the remainder of the program. As you move from phase to phase, you will need to make this part of your program. Every project has risk associated with it, and it comes in many forms that you need to constantly be aware of. The following list shows some of these risks.

- *Resources.* It is natural to have resource constraints. Make sure that you are managing and flagging the resource constraints well in advance of this becoming an issue.
- *Talent.* You must hire the right people with the right skill sets for the job.
- *Time lines.* Do you have imposed deadlines instead of planned deadlines?
- *Vacations/Holidays/People leaving.* These impact projects every day.
- *External, global, third-party teams.* Time zones, distances, cultures, languages, and diversity are all risk.

Not planning for an upcoming task is a risk. Not having a plan and following that plan end to end is a risk. What are all the changes you are making and have you planned for the outcomes of the changes?

The better you understand what risks there are and address those risks, the more successful your program will be. Although we are just touching on risk management, do not make the mistake of overlooking this part of the program.

Pitfalls

- Not organizing the requirements into a one pager, two to four-page document, and, finally, a detailed technical specs that can be a hundred or more pages
- Not including the IT evangelist in the BRD process
- Not identifying all the right subject-matter experts that should be involved in this project
- Not documenting future-state processes
- Not identifying all of the roles and responsibilities that will be impacted by this project
- Not having the right people write the BRD

Fundamentals and executive support continue to take the majority of your time. Planning, finance planning, and implementing change management are each strong focal points in this chapter. Team structure remains a point of consideration, and Rescue/recovery requires minimal attention.

CHAPTER 7

IT DATA: THE FOUNDATION

Symptoms

- Trouble gaining adoption or selling and promoting the technical solution because the business does not understand the technical terms being presented
- Governance and ownership issues exist—lack of centralized data and processes
- End solution not sustainable, repeatable, or transferable to other areas/applications/businesses
- Project team not sure where all the data comes from and whether it has been manipulated before or after they work with it

Business Integration of New Role of Business Analyst

Finding the right person to fill the role of *technology evangelist* who possesses the right skill set and core competencies is vital. You want someone who will work with the project manager from the business to develop the right solution for the program. Although some people are outstanding technology developers, it is important to make sure the person you choose also has outstanding communication skills. She must also have the ability to understand and interpret the needs of the business in order to create the right solution.

The technology evangelist must be in alignment with the business-process owners. This person should possess the skills needed to communicate and understand the complexities and needs of the business. Miscommunication at this stage will possibly kill the program.

The technology evangelist needs to have the right skill set, core competencies, knowledge, technical skills, vision, ability, and drive to carry this project forward. You need to find the person with the overall knowledge and abilities to understand and be able to carry out the complexities of the project.

The technology evangelist should have the best technology skill set and the ability to communicate ideas and goals to the technology side of the business. This person must not only be able to understand the business's goals and vision but also be able to translate the program to the technology side. It is only through this relationship that the two sides will work together with a clear, workable understanding of what is to be achieved.

The technology evangelist must have a complete understanding of the vision and current state of the business to help formulate the future state. In order to do this, the person must have a complete, end-to-end knowledge of the current-state processes as well as the vision of the future state. Keep in mind that telling a person what the vision is is not the same as him understanding it. This understanding takes time, and daily communication is a must if you want things to work.

The technology evangelist must be a change catalyst. The team must drive the solution forward. They will coordinate and direct the enterprise architects, business systems architects, engineers, and developers. All of these people will be centralized to this team and must be coordinated in order to achieve success.

Centralize Data within the Team

Once you have identified the architects for the program, you must determine whether the technology evangelist and the data manipulators are centralized under this program. By going through the following steps, you will have a good understanding of the status of the team.

- Have centralized data within the team.
- Tie the technology evangelist to the businessperson working within the business.
- Have control over the data.
- Have a data flow that is fully defined and mapped out.
- Have all the calculations validated, approved, and published.
- Set up the foundation correctly to achieve the strategic objectives.
- Have a "cave" the team can work from.

One of the core tenants of your program will be information flows. Everyone on the team should share and agree on the vision of the process. They need to have a core knowledge and clear understanding of the process that will be used to achieve the vision. Constant, real-time communication will be the program's lifesaver. You must have daily communication among the team members in order to keep everyone on track. Do not let assumptions get in the way of the success of the program.

The technology evangelist must be tied to a point person working within the business. He should have real-time access to the business when needed. This real-time communication will ensure that all parties are on the same page and moving in the same direction. If constant, easy access between the technology evangelist and the business is not set up and available, deviations and separation of goals and ideas are going to occur and may derail the program.

Another precaution to take is making sure you have control over the data. Make sure you have a single version of the truth. Having consistent, reliable data flows that are fully defined and mapped out is a critical step that enables you to accurately validate, approve, and publish all the calculations. This will ensure the validity of data for all phases of the program.

You need to correctly set up the data foundation to achieve the strategic objectives. You want to make sure that realistic goals and objectives are clearly communicated for the program. A priority matrix can be a critical tool. You will tie the priority matrix to the features and function-alities, and then tie these to the cost-benefit analysis.

As stated before, it is desirable to establish a "cave" for your team to work in. This is an area, apart from others, in which the team can work. You want team members to be on-site and accessible to each other. This not only creates a cohesive work environment but also allows for instant issue resolution and idea flows. There's not a time lag in trying to con-nect with people who are scattered around the office or, worse, around the world. Issue resolution can become a nightmare with technology if you use the scatter approach for teams. Keeping your team centralized can be a huge advantage.

Blending Business Process into Technology

You need to blend the business into the technology to form a seamless process that is scalable, repeatable, and transferable. In order to do this, you will need to utilize work flows, process flow alerts, and automate. You want to create a cloud-based solution in which all of the data is con-nected and validated. There are companies offering great solutions uti-lizing IaaS, PaaS, and SaaS options with business intelligence, machine learning, and a host of other services.

The process tasks should be designed and built into the work flows wherever possible and also automated, leaving the data analysis to the business analyst. The nonanalytical tasks should be done by machine whenever possible. The goal is to eliminate all of the human steps and automate the entire process.

Documenting Current- to Future-State Technical Flows

Technical flows should be completed the same as process flows. This be-comes more important as your program becomes more complex. When you have one or two data sources, this may not be a problem. In large companies, however, you can have programs that incorporate fifty to one hundred applications or more. The complexities that you run into with these types of programs can be very high, and having data-flow diagrams can be critical. You can have resources working on these programs who are experts in only one application and do not see the big picture. Even having data flows does not ensure you will be successful, but it does increase your odds. Much of the success depends on the solution architect who is working on the solution.

Pitfalls

- Not hiring an IT business analyst who is a change catalyst
- Not integrating the data into a single area for this team to define and control—a single source of truth
- Not incorporating or automating business processes into technology (work flows)
- Not documenting/validating the entire data flow, current state to future state end to end

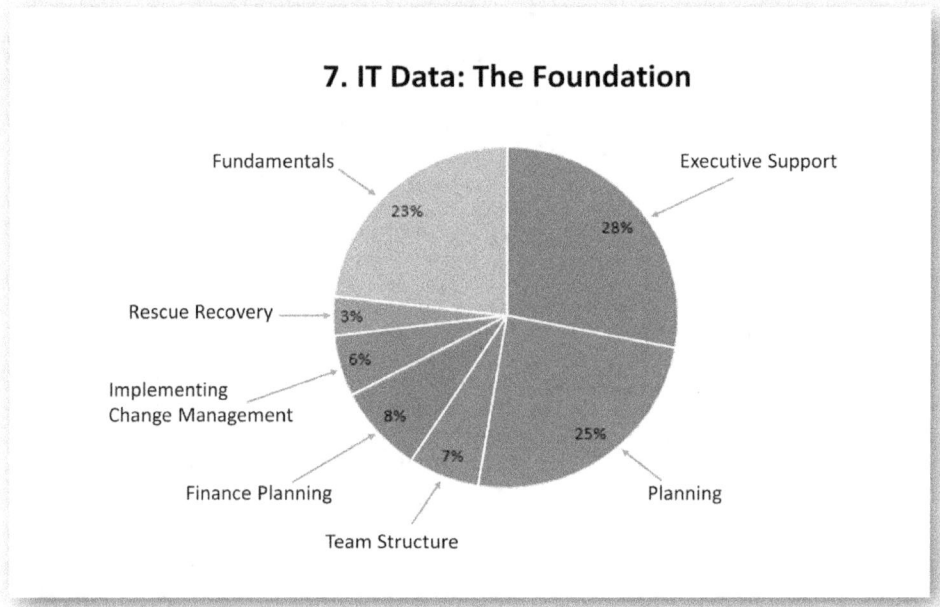

7. IT Data: The Foundation

Executive support and fundamentals remain the focus of your time in chapter 7. The time allotment for planning has increased at this phase. Finance planning, team structure, and implementing change management have each decreased their time allotment, with rescue/recovery increasing its focus slightly.

CHAPTER 8

DEFINE THE FRAMEWORK

Symptoms

- Confusion on the project and business side about what structure will be used to complete the project
- Constant issues and a lack of resolution of the issues
- No development priority list created, resources skills unknown, dependencies/impacts unclear
- Unknown development resource needs
- Executives questioning the benefits of the project
- Lack of organization and team definition or documentation—no executive approval
- People uncertain about what their changing roles will become
- Resources overallocated for projects
- Oh-no moments happening close to launch—escalations of issues occurring
- Constantly changing launch dates
- Functional groups have lack of concern about launch

Symptoms of the Framework Not Being Defined

- No milestones created
- Lack of common structure that all parties understand
- No commitment to the project until it is launched
- Lack of understanding of what is being launched
- Lack of written documentation of what is being launched
- Lack of concern about the launch

Symptoms of Time Lines and Deliverables Not Being Complete

- Constantly changing milestone and launch dates
- Escalations of issues
- Short tempers
- Not talking to the business
- Panic moments occurring as the launch date nears
- Constant issues and a lack of addressing the issues
- Allowing the business to drive the time line

Part of the strategy when doing a project is picking a framework. This is where the *Business Strategy for Success* comes in handy as a complete strategy rather than as a partial solution. Some of the tools that can be used are traditional Six Sigma, Lean, Waterfall, SDLC, and Agile as well as others, including self-defined methods. The important thing is to pick a framework and make sure everyone is in agreement and alignment with the structure. It becomes more difficult when you're at a place that is transitioning from one framework to another and you are working somewhere in between the two frameworks. This transition causes all kinds of problems, especially as companies move from traditional Waterfall or SDLC to Agile. Waterfall and SDLC contain all the structure you have defined. Agile, however, is more of an art form in which groups will function differently from each other and that is okay. It is natural for management to think that all groups should operate exactly the same. At a high level, the framework is the same, but how the teams operate can vary greatly. I would like to introduce the priority matrix, which is a lesser-known tool that, used in the right way, can be extremely beneficial.

There are a couple of things to know in advance. One is that the priority matrix will be the map of everything you need to do to build the process. The more detailed and complete it is, the more smoothly your project will run. It is an involved process that will need to be done without a lot of interruption. You should not view this as a part-time task. You should have a dedicated team working to complete the priority matrix. The other is that the person working on the priority matrix will need to have active participation from the IT project lead. Working together, the business lead and the IT lead will use the BDR to ensure that all of the functionalities needed for the initiative are being undertaken. You want communication flows between all partners in order to clarify questions and discuss possible additions or changes.

When you are done, you will have the following:

- a validated document that, if delivered, both IT and the business agree will create the intent of the initiative;
- a list of features and functionalities ordered to show the sequence build and the subsequent delivery;
- a list of features and functionalities along with the dependencies that are required to be completed in order for delivery;
- a document that the business and project manager will use to align the features and functionalities with the CBA, which was created for this initiative (the project plan created within the priority matrix will be assessable where man-hour determinations will be made);

- identification of resource needs and availability scaling before any work begins (with the priority matrix, IT will be able to prioritize and schedule resources and development);
- an executive scorecard that will detail specific feature and functionality time lines as well as CBA delivery estimates; and
- an established collaboration across all of the functional participants in creating the priority matrix to ensure that everyone is recognizing and working to solve the same issues.

Once you have completed this process, the priority matrix will become the single working document that everyone will work from. It will replace the BRD, SRS, IT project plan, CBA, and resource tracker.

Building the Priority Matrix

The first objective to building the priority matrix is to lift all the features and functionality out of the business-requirement documents. The goal is to create a more workable, organized format. You want to start by listing all of the functionality and features that are being requested for this initiative.

During this exercise, you will create a traceability matrix. The functionality buckets are high-level detail. They will not document the specific details of the features involved. You will need to capture the feature, detailed description, value or benefiting group, and dependencies (if any) needing delivery prior to this feature being developed. You will also need to identify what other features are dependent on this initiative. We suggest you use a tab in Excel for each functionality bucket.

Once you have completed the traceability matrix, you will lift each functionality bucket out, along with the features associated with it, into a new document. Now you are ready to begin building the priority matrix.

Each feature will be grouped into a functionality bucket.

Example compensation functionality buckets for priority matrix

Pay Process	Bucket	Compensation Views	Bucket	Compensation Setup Process	Bucket
Display and archive contest rules	Pay process	Group content by sales team or business	Segmentation	Establish support team for each sales team or business	Setup
Work with payroll to validate pay file format and content	Pay process	Sales rep view	Segmentation	Refine process as applicable to each business	Setup
Consolidate sales reporting into payroll formats	Pay process	Manager view	Segmentation	Gain executive buy in to support all core compensation roles	Setup
Consolidate all sales rep pay out gates and qualifiers	Pay process	Regional sales manager view	Segmentation	Create and manage the vendor funding process	Setup

Once you've completed the task of lifting every feature out of the BDR and mapping it to a functionality bucket, you will walk through and review every bucket with the key owners and representatives to ensure that every feature is captured. At this point, it is critical to confirm the understanding and development needs of every feature. Refer to the traceability matrix as needed to confirm your understanding of the features and functionalities. From this, the IT lead may need to break features into multiple steps.

Once you are confident that you have a complete list of features from each functionality bucket that need development, you will list the features in each bucket in the order that they need to be developed to deliver that functionality bucket. Upon completion of ordering the features for each functionality bucket, you will put your first pass of a priority matrix together. This will include information from both the traceability matrix and the list ordering you have completed. You will list the features and functionality buckets in a single list along with their individual orderings.

Then, you will merge the **Dependency** and **Required for** columns from the traceability matrix so that within the priority matrix you will now have **Bucket rank**, **Feature**, **Bucket dependency**, and **Required for** as your column headings. Finally, this list will be ordered, taking into account dependencies, to show a listing of what needs to be built and the order in which it should be done.

Example compensation priority matrix with build order

Development Order	Bucket Rank	Development Task	Bucket	Dependency	Required For
1	1	House all reporting results within a single database	Manual Process Support	Business Integration Process	
2	1	Group functionality and content by sales team or business	Segmentation	Application plus database enhancement	Segmented data and content management
3	1	Segmented view of total compensation spend with pay	Budgets	Business Integration process, application plus database enhancement	Financial tracking and reconcile budget
4	2	Interface with business metrics tools for rep level data	Business metrics integration	Identify business metrics, frequency of data availability	Sales rep view, Metric availability for contest calculation
5	2	Provide direct link and visibility to key business metrics	Manual Process Support	Business metrics integration	Sales rep view, Metric availability for contest calculation

From here, you will add the CBA benefits as features that are completed. Development leads will now realize the order of the work needed and be able to staff and prioritize accordingly. Extremely specific project plans can be easily created based on this order of development.

Priority Matrix Planning

In the process of building this, you should not change the people on the team. If you do, you should start over. If you have the wrong people, you cannot change them into the right people.

In chapter 7, you did a review of all the elements covered in chapters 1 through 7, making sure that you completed all the steps, processes, documents, and people. Now, you want to check everything to date to ensure that you are ready to launch. If everything is not complete, you should not launch at this time. The priority matrix will validate this for you. As you complete it, both the business and IT leads will work through all of the features and functionalities to ensure that there are no gaps in the understanding of what is to be accomplished.

IT Planning

The priority matrix will help IT to prioritize and schedule resources and development. The highlighted dependencies will allow you to explain when things will be developed and why they are to be developed in the order in which they have been ranked.

Align Features to CBA

It is important to align the priority matrix to the CBA. You will use this as an executive scorecard—a measurable reference—for the executives' benefit of understanding.

Change Management Planning

The priority matrix will manage the changes in the business. Who, what, and when the changes occur will be thoroughly documented.

The following are issues that pertain to change management.

- Communicate to the executives. Critical executives as well as business leads have to understand that the priority matrix is the blueprint for how the process will be built and delivered. Do not underestimate the importance of this communication.
- Define the new organization. You must have built out the new organizational structure as well as roles and responsibilities.
- Define the new team and what it will look like.
- Outline clearly. What is it, who does it, when does it happen, and why is it being done? If the answers to these questions are not defined, you are not ready to continue.

Time-in-Motion Study

This should be completed with forecasting for the coming launch included. You should have all of the roles and responsibilities included that will be changed as the process change is implemented along with the interim roles and responsibilities.

Risk Analysis

Risk analysis is keeping track of all risk to the project and of the mitigation plans to be implemented if the risk cannot be overcome. A common example of risk is resources overallocated for projects. If the project becomes bogged down because you have only one developer, who is on multiple projects with similar time lines, you may have to get executives involved to prioritize the projects as well as the developer's time. You may also need to rebaseline the project if it is deemed to be of a lower priority. Keeping a constant eye on risk is key to keeping the project on track. You have risk every day whether you acknowledge it or not.

Time Lines and Deliverables (Deployment Prep)

As you approach the program launch and have completed the priority matrix, there are issues you need to consider to determine whether your timelines and deliverables are complete. You should

- have a good project management/deployment lead;
- work with all of the functional groups to get agreement on all the time lines and deliverables;
- set reasonable expectations with the business and all functional partners;
- work toward a launch based on completing the foundation and deliverables to ensure a successful program;
- have development testing, system testing, vendor testing (if applicable), and user-acceptance test plans completed and approved;
- have validation of the business process complete and approved;
- have all new processes documented, tested, and validated by the business;
- make sure all parties know their roles and responsibilities;
- complete check of all steps and the oh-no moments that occur prior to launch;
- have completed all of the previous steps;
- secure a support structure set up for prelaunch (one to two months prior);

- secure a support structure set up for post launch (one to three months after);
- work with all of the functional groups on a daily basis to address their questions, concerns, and issues; and
- make a list of the top issues you are likely to face, along with outlines and plans to fix them, including contacts and people in the war room ready to resolve all issues.

The Deployment Plan

To creating the deployment plan,

- have daily questions you are addressing and working through with the business,
- plan the time lines and deliverables,
- have a rollback plan prior to launch, and
- have business integration occurring at its highest level prior to launch.

You now have the priority matrix and the team. It is time to access both and get accountability to time lines and deliverables.

- Assess whether training is needed.
- Identify whether you have the right people.
- Determine whether the team is committed.
- Secure IT development.
- Work daily with the business.
  - Agile development—works well with the priority matrix. Again, this is subjective and may not work for every environment.
  - Scrum—daily basis working on what can be achieved today from an IT deliverable basis.
  - Business/IT evangelist—working with the business daily to get people involved and excited. You need to have access daily, weekly, or as needed.

Make sure the risk-assessment plan is complete as well as being worked on daily as things change.

Go- or No-Go Call

Plans for the launch are usually prepared four to six weeks in advance of the launch. The go or no-go call is made as you approach the launch date. If any of the steps are not complete, questions are not answered, or you have a lack of communication and commitment, you have a no-go! These issues must be addressed. This meeting is usually held one week in advance of the launch date, with issues being worked out during this time and a final go or no-go call made days before the launch.

Pitfalls

- Not picking a framework that IT and the business are both using together and both agree on
- Not evaluating the project and not picking the right framework for that project
- Not completing the priority matrix
- Not identifying development resource needs for the project
- Not creating an executive scorecard
- Not having a change-management plan
- Not fully defining the new roles and responsibilities for each team member and not integrating the team daily on their new roles
- Not creating a risk-assessment plan
- Not having a good deployment lead
- Not creating a deployment plan
- Not including all stakeholders in the go or no-go meeting

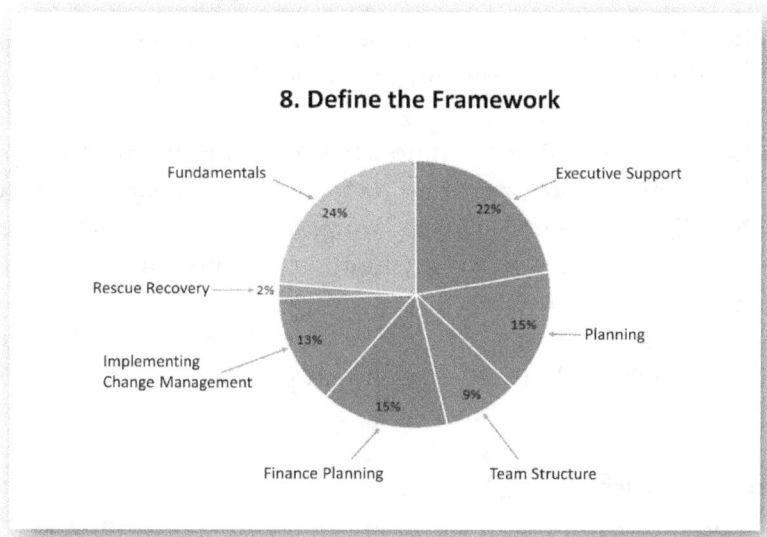

8. Define the Framework

Fundamentals and executive support continue to hold the greatest focus. Planning, finance planning, and implementing change management follow, with team structure and rescue/recovery remaining considerations.

CHAPTER 9

BUSINESS INTEGRATION

Symptoms

- People confused as to what their changing roles will become
- Confusion around roles and responsibilities—gaps occur in tasks coverage
- Deterioration of cooperation between the project team and all functional parties as the project team pushes back on ownership
- No alignment between what you got and what you expected
- Project launches to no excitement or general lack of engagement from the business
- No adoption of new process by the business, while project team disengages and moves on to the next project

Business Integration Defined

Business integration is the comprehensive, coordinated change of your business process. By this point, you should have identified and mapped out all of the business's integration points—the points at which change is occurring. This will be a review and preparation for the deployment. If you deploy in phases, all points will be fully defined and communicated to all parties so that everyone is clear on their involvement in the project plan.

The following points will vary by role. The primary person will be the change catalyst performing these actions. If you are not a change catalyst, you may question whether you should be.

- Are you performing this throughout the project?
- Are you performing this with every new person to the project?
- Are you performing this daily with the core team?
- Are you performing this with all of the functional groups?
- Are you the change catalyst for the project?
- Can you define the change catalyst's role and responsibility?
- What groups do you work with in the business integration?
- Is change management getting off of the previous system?
- Have you defined all of the interim plans and roles and responsibilities as well as processes?

You will need to have plans for every phase of the program, including the final phase.

Deployment of the Program (Support Model Defined)

When you've reached the deployment stage, the following model will assist you in making sure you are staying on top of the strategy.

- You have executive support.
- Key milestones with the CBA tied to the deployment plan will continue to foster executive buy in and support.
- Make sure that all changes are fully communicated and supported.
- The key executive should lead the change management and display their full support.
- New processes will be defined along with the time stamp of when they are integrated and implemented into the system.
- New processes are fully mapped and defined.
- New core competencies are defined.

- New people and teams are in place.
- Interim roles and responsibilities are understood and in place.

Another issue that needs to be considered is the vision. The project plan needs to be reviewed to confirm that you are in alignment with the original intent (vision) of the process that was defined at the beginning of the program. This should tie directly back to the original strategy statement that was created at the beginning.

These are the management-of-change items:

- people,
- business structure,
- reorganizations,
- management,
- scope change,
- deployment,
- user acceptance testing, and
- system testing IT.

Business Adoption of the Program

If you have followed all of the steps outlined, you should have full support and adoption of the program by the business. But if you're experiencing pushback by the business, it may be an indicator that you have overlooked or even omitted key subject-matter experts, stakeholders, or functionalities. If this is the case, you must move quickly and overcommunicate to understand what the issues are. The longer these issues are ignored, the more difficult it will be to resolve them and move forward. You cannot bulldoze the business through the issues without resolution. This will only lead to conflict and possibly the failure to move forward with the new program.

Stabilization of the Program

If you have a best-case scenario, you have followed, absolutely, the steps and have outlined every aspect and issue that can occur. You are ready!

But, more often than not, you will be trying to stabilize a program that has issues you have not planned for. This will occur when you don't identify all of the subject-matter experts or you did not fully understand the current state of the business. In stabilizing, you must fully understand the current state of the business and map out the current-state processes and put them into buckets:

- items to be automated,
- items that require a business-process or methodology change or that are no longer necessary to do, and
- items that will continue to be done using existing process or methodology.

Redefining Business Processes

You want to make sure that all of the new processes are valid, accurate, and ready to hand over to the business in the form in which they were developed. A thorough review and sign-off by the business is essential. You need to verify that the business understands the new processes and that they are educated to run them properly.

To ensure that the business will be properly trained, you will create work instructions on a step-by-step scale for every process change. It is important that you make sure the business is trained and knows how to use the new processes. Unfortunately, this step is sometimes left out. The process team moves on to its new program before fully training the business, and you end up with a process that will fail or be underutilized. This can lead to the business being unsatisfied and looking for something new to replace what you have built.

Business Sign-Off

The business should have complete work instructions and process maps with roles and responsibilities completed prior to the sign-off. Only after this is complete and everything works should the business sign off on the program.

Pitfalls

- Not hiring a change catalyst to drive the project
- Underestimating the importance of managing organizational, process, and role changes
- Not creating a solid change-management plan
- Assuming the business will evolve to the right solution
- Not working daily with the business to make sure it understands its new role and responsibilities and that all current-state tasks have been accounted for and moved into three buckets (process is automated, the business has been changed and the process is no longer needed, or this process will continue to be done as is)
- Not having a change catalyst at all levels to help drive the project changes

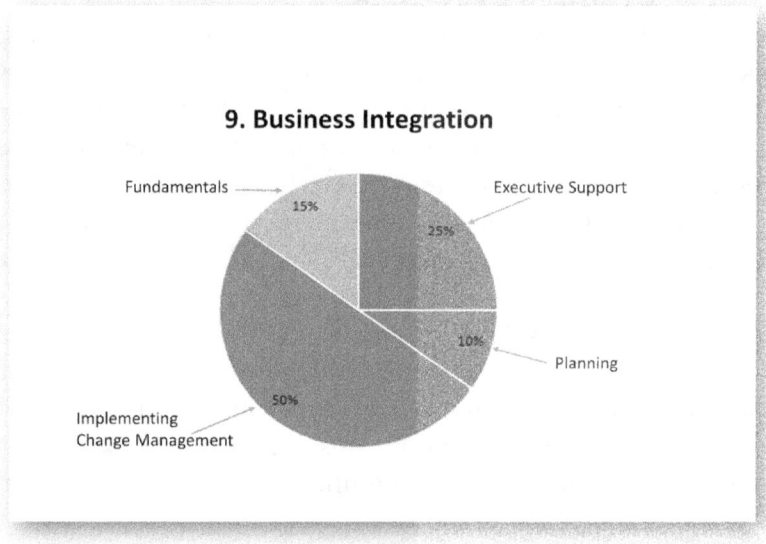

Implementing change management has increased dramatically at this phase. Executive support remains an important component. Fundamentals has dropped considerably, with planning falling to a smaller time allotment as well.

CHAPTER 10

MEASURE AND FUTURE STATE

Symptoms

- No way of identifying the impact of the launch—ambiguity of success measure or criteria
- Different groups involved in the launch all have different definitions of success with no way to reconcile the overall success of the project
- Broad statements by individuals of success of the project with no measureable details to back it up
- Project team has gone on to next project

Measuring the Success or Failure of the Program

One of the most important tools that should be built into your program is the ability to measure the success or failure of the program you are building. If you have followed each step and built out everything required in these steps, you will have your measure and validation. Consider the following bullet points to validate your program.

- Refer back to your strategy from chapter 1. Pull out the paragraph you completed in which you outlined your strategy—the future state or the bulls-eye. Did you accomplish your goal? Did you stay true to the true vision of the program?

Compensation Example

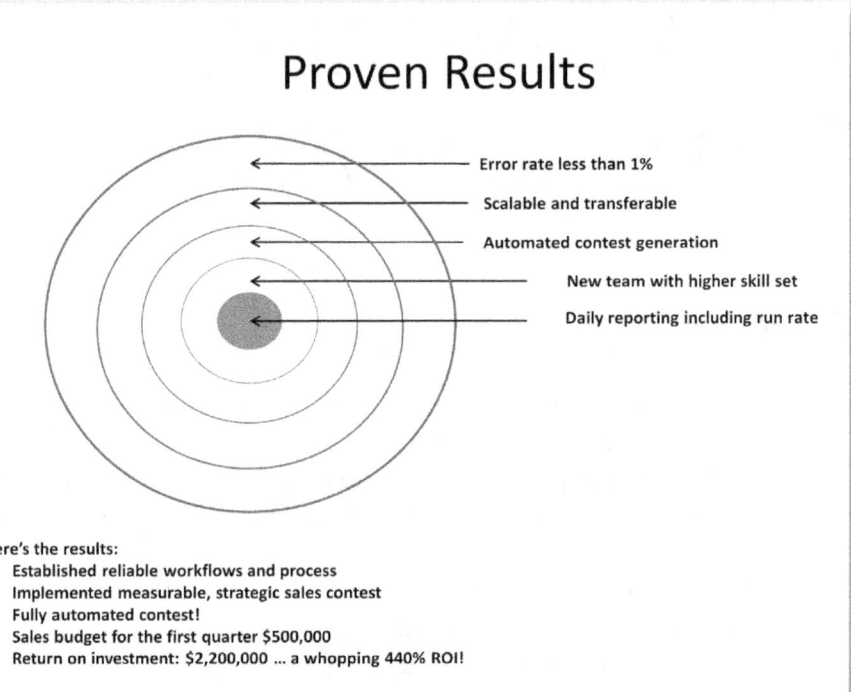

Proven Results

- Error rate less than 1%
- Scalable and transferable
- Automated contest generation
- New team with higher skill set
- Daily reporting including run rate

Here's the results:
- Established reliable workflows and process
- Implemented measurable, strategic sales contest
- Fully automated contest!
- Sales budget for the first quarter $500,000
- Return on investment: $2,200,000 ... a whopping 440% ROI!

- Refer to the time-in-motion study. This will be validated by the business and will be your ongoing measure to keep track of future work and enhancements to the program. You should now be able to put together, for the executive team, the actual savings of the program. You will create efficiencies and reduce people, processes, error rates, and other variables before, during, and after the program is completed.

Example Compensation Time-in-Motion Study

The final portion should be completed postdeployment of the new process, giving you a new look at the process results.

Time in Motion Study

	Prior to launch manual process	Post launch automated process
Error Rate	>15%	<1%
Number of times sales reports are run monthly	1	30
Average number of reports run monthly	60	60
Time it takes to set up and run sales reports	30 plus days	30 seconds
Increased revenue	$0	$2,200,000 or a 440% increase in revenue
Total headcount to support the program	8	1 Business analyst

- Refer to the CBA. Financial impacts should be validated by the finance controller and measured for success. This is a consolidation of all the cost benefits, including the time-in-Motion study that will take all of the measures you have provided in your strategy statement. This should be reviewed by all executive sponsors to validate profitability and the success of the program.

Other impacts that should be validated by the business are cost avoidance, efficiencies, and automation.

Defining the Business-Analyst Role as It Fits with Business Intelligence

Once the program is complete, the business-analyst role becomes even more critical. At this point, the BA has control of all data from beginning to end. This enables the BA to analyze the data and perform the role she was hired for. She can now make recommendations based on the pure data. There are many BA roles, but not many BAs can analyze the data and make the necessary recommendations to the business's executives.

This role will define

- what you measure and why,
- how you utilize the data,
- automation of the reporting,
- standardization of reporting,
- business intelligence, and
- return on investment.

Future State of the Program

We're done. Many programs end with the deployment of the program. The project team moves to the next project, executive support goes away, and no further thought goes into the program. This can be a fatal flaw in the way some projects are run.

You want to evaluate the accomplishments of the program. Again, look through all of the steps of the program to see what was accomplished, and identify the specific items that worked well to make sure you replicate that in the next program. Lessons learned can be critical to not making the same mistakes over and over.

Just as you want to evaluate your accomplishments, you must analyze and evaluate the failures in the project as well. Taking the time to analyze why something failed will enable you to identify the issues in real time, as they occur. For example, by evaluating your failures, you may find that issues arose because of steps being skipped in the project in order to save time. Your analysis may reveal that you actually added time because you had to go back and resolve issues that arose as a result of the skipped steps. By learning from past mistakes and understanding them, you will enable your team to make better decisions that will enhance all future projects.

This methodology requires utilization of many different disciplines as well as years of actual experience. Even then, you are learning on a daily basis. You have to be open to listening to the input of all people at all levels and then sifting through to understand what is relevant and how to apply it to your project.

You must also plan for the next phase. Rarely do you have a project start and finish with only a single effort. Most projects are run with little or no thought to reviewing what the next steps are. If you recall the introduction, there are many handoffs and different groups and people that usually perform the steps in a project. The work you do in this chapter will help you identify what direction needs to be taken going forward. Keeping the project teams together and compensating them based on the success of the project will spur the team to continue to innovate and keep improving the solution. Once you stop innovating, you are falling behind. Companies that are not continually improving will fall by the wayside and be consumed by the companies that are hungry and want to change. Change is not something that most people or companies are comfortable with. A good project team can continue to make the business work more efficiently and effectively.

I hope you've gotten some useful information from *Business Strategy for Success*. It's a system that I use daily, not only for business but also in my personal life. I've even taught it to my kids, who have used it, with great success, for college projects as well as independent projects that they have worked on.

The key is organization and accountability.

Pitfalls

- Not defining how you will measure the success of the project (quantifiable, measureable, and conservative)
- Not aligning the success criteria to the strategic initiatives of the company
- Not hiring a business analyst with the right skill sets to manage/own the data and measure the project's success
- Thinking the project is complete and no other work is needed

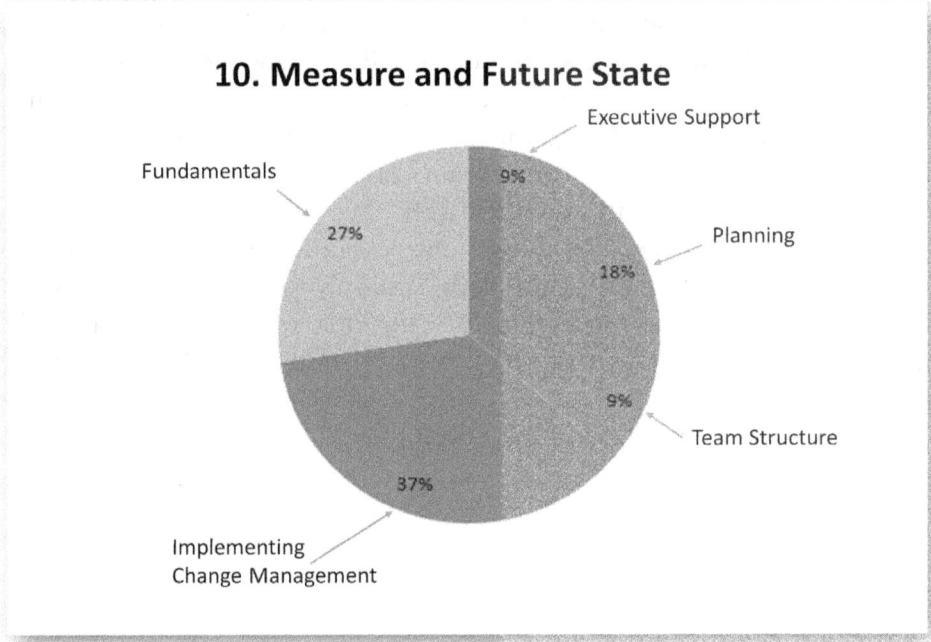

10. Measure and Future State

Executive Support 9%

Fundamentals 27%

Planning 18%

Team Structure 9%

Implementing Change Management 37%

Implementing change management and fundamentals are strong factors in this chapter. Planning will continue to garner attention, and executive support and team structure will require consideration as well.

FINAL NOTE

Included with the *Business Strategy for Success* is the maturity model and an explanation on how to know where your business is in order to align it for long-term improvement. *Business Strategy for Success* is a discipline designed to run successful projects. By learning this system, you will find that you continue to improve your success with every project you do. The steps you utilize will become an integral part of your daily project experience. The steps should, in time, become intuitive, as you will learn to anticipate steps or issues before they actually occur. You will begin to work in a proactive manner rather than in a defensive mode.

By utilizing the *Business Strategy for Success* throughout the scope of all of your business's projects, you will find that your placement on the maturity model will rise. Your teams will become a better-working unit because they will understand the discipline you are using regardless of the framework being used.

This is what is so exciting about this system. It crosses the realm of frameworks. It gives your business the stability of a sustainable, repeatable system. Although the maturity model goes beyond the scope of this book, those who are familiar with this model will understand how following the steps outlined in *Business Strategy for Success* will help you achieve consistently higher rankings on the maturity model scale.

APPENDIX A

Maturity Model—Knowing Where You Are

It is difficult to make progress if you do not know where you are in relation to where you are going. The maturity model helps to align businesses on long-term process improvement.

	Maturity Level	Criteria
"Automating" Business Process & BI	6 - - - ▶ "Automation"	▪ Automated Alerts/Resolution ▪ Automated business process guidance ▪ Self Reliance
Understanding BI	5 "Optimizing"	▪ Processes are Analyzed, optimized and adjusted to changes in market requirements systematically ▪ Benchmarking and Best Practice Sharing are used continuously in order to identify improvement potential. ▪ Methods for mistake avoidance are used
	4 "Quantitatively Managed"	▪ Continuous measurement and adjustment of process performance ▪ Process management is constantly accessed an improved ▪ Initiatives are managed with quality planning and implementation
"Doing" Brute force Manual Process	3 "Defined"	▪ The process is defined, adopted and utilized by all functional groups. ▪ A comprehensible assessment and prioritization of these processes is conducted ▪ Responsibilities for processes are established (roles, committees, approvals, prioritization, etc.) ▪ Rules and methods of the process management are defined and implemented
	2 "Managed"	▪ The need for action is identified. Project manager is entitled to direct the functional businesses ▪ Some of the processes are standardized ▪ Process management is needed ▪ Situational approach for managing projects is utilized. No standard framework is used.
	1 "Initial"	▪ Processes are not defined – ad-hoc approach ▪ Success depends on certain specialists or SME's ▪ Schedule, quality and costs are not predictable

Many companies never get out of step 1, and fewer get past step 2. That being the case, most businesses will be in a constant state of churn, will remain resource intensive, and will not mature to the point of being able to add business intelligence to their programs or projects. Even fewer companies will ever complete step 3.

If you look at the left-hand side of the diagram, you will note that the first three steps of the maturity model are very resource intensive. Start-ups do not have the money or directives to look at a maturity model. Their focus is solely to get a revenue stream. Midsize companies tend to delegate projects to people with the bandwidth to get things done and also do not have a great deal budgeted to spend on specialists, so they also may not be looking at maturity models. Large companies do have a budget, however, and they also have the most to gain from long-term process improvement. It is to their benefit to understand the maturity model, and it is essential to long-term business enhancement. It can be overwhelming in the sense that the maturity model applies not only to one department that you are in but also to every department in a company.

Maturity Model: Steps 1, 2, and 3

Businesses must complete steps 1, 2, and 3 before they can graduate to business intelligence. Many times, however, these steps are skipped and the business intelligence that is gathered is not relevant, since garbage in almost always equals garbage out. The end result is that decisions are made on bad data, which ultimately ends in consequences that can be detrimental to the business. Oftentimes, the symptom is masked by constant reorganizations that do not allow for the changes to be realized.

Sometimes companies will add the SDLC framework and give the illusion that because the development team can develop a product, the product is viable. The first half of the project still has to be completed, and there is no formal process for the business to do this. Adding structure to only half of the life cycle eliminates the traditional target on the IT side. SDLC focuses more on the execution of developing software and not the delivery of the strategy.

Maturity Model: Steps 4 and 5

Once the first three steps are a standard for the company, you can move on to step 4, in which you have the ability to measure the results of your efforts. In this phase, your business analysts will gain an understanding of all the data, end to end. They will understand who touches the data and any manipulations that occur. Ideally, the data is pure, with no changes or interpretations of the data between the initial extraction or gathering of data and the actual analysis. It is easy to lose perspective of where you are in the model if the data is manipulated prior to the analyst receiving it.

Step 5 is the second piece of understanding business intelligence. Now that the analyst has control of the data, and it is not being manipulated by anyone, you can read the data and make recommendations to the business. This is the point at which you can evaluate raw data, read the trends, and, with modeling and educated assumptions, drive the business. You can uncover trends that may have been used for years but may actually be detrimental to the business. Constant change is often a symptom of negative trends (possibly due to data manipulation) that lead to bad habits, and it is something to always be aware of.

Maturity Model: Step 6

Although not a major point covered in this book, automation of both business processes and business intelligence is not only possible but will be the future. Automation of business processes includes templates to complete for every step of each process, with instructions, examples, time lines, approvals, and alerts to all relevant parties that are a part of the business today. The same can be done with business intelligence. Automation means starting out with assumptions but gaining intelligence as you go. With every run through the process, you learn things to categorize, such as the size of the program, the complexity, and the number of functional partners involved. This will help drive toward a standard deviation for like programs and thus give you parameters that can be adjusted for any program. You will have the ability to fine-tune or dial into the projects and understand, in real time, where you have issues, giving the team and the executives the opportunity to address these issues early. This ultimately leads to machine learning, which is here now and quickly advancing. These truly are exciting times.

Author Bio

R ussell Freytag has over twenty years of experience working as both an employee and consultant in a wide range of business settings, including Fortune 50 companies, state and local governmental agencies, and start-ups. He has been on both the business and IT sides of creating and working with various initiatives.

Freytag specializes in tackling firsts for companies, taking on ventures that others do not have the skill to execute or are unwilling to approach due to risk. He has coached corporate executives on business strategy, operations, and methodology. As a consultant, he has taken on the restructuring, streamlining, and design of departments, initiatives, and entire companies and agencies.